When Hope Is All You Have is a must-read for anyone who has ever questioned the goodness of God and His plans for them and their family. My dear friends Tracy and Troy Duhon have gone through ruthless trials, grief, loss, and trauma that could have caused them to believe God isn't real. However, when you see how beautifully God brought miraculous strength and purposes through the shattered pieces, it is undeniable evidence and a testimony of God's ultimate care for each of us.

God is good. God is awesome. God is real. Not only will this book encourage you and stir up faith; it will minister to the depths of your soul, as we all wonder at times where God is in our time of need. I can't imagine what this has been like for Tracy and Troy—a million times more difficult than being born without limbs!

Yet we see how God can cause *all* things to come together for the good of those who love Him and have been called according to His purposes. This book will challenge your faith and bring a renewed sense of God's faithfulness in your life!

—NICK VUJICIC
AUTHOR AND SPEAKER

This is an anointed work. Read every page. *When Hope Is All You Have* is both heartbreaking and hope filled. This book is powerfully written—we couldn't put it down!

Thank you, Tracy and Troy Duhon, for sharing

your deeply devastating, raw journey through the crucible of losing not only one but two sons. This work has deepened our personal faith and hope in the constant companionship of our God.

When Hope Is All You Have is fresh. It will deepen your trust and challenge you to surrender even more of your life to the King of kings! What a tremendous gift of *hope* it is to each one of us, showing us that God can be fully trusted in every situation.

—Dr. Gary and Barbara Rosberg
Cofounders, America's Family Coaches;
Authors, *6 Secrets to a Lasting Love*

When HOPE Is All You Have

TRACY DUHON

CHARISMA HOUSE

The author has made every effort to provide accurate accounts of events, but she acknowledges that others may have different recollections of these events.

While the author has made every effort to provide accurate, up-to-date source information at the time of publication, statistics and other data are constantly updated. Neither the publisher nor the author assumes any responsibility for errors or for changes that occur after publication. Further, the publisher and author do not have any control over and do not assume any responsibility for third-party websites or their content.

For more resources like this, visit charismahouse.com and the author's website at tracyduhon.com.

Cataloging-in-Publication Data is on file with the Library of Congress.
International Standard Book Number: 978-1-63641-353-2
E-book ISBN: 978-1-63641-354-9

1 2024
Printed in the United States of America

Most Charisma Media products are available at special quantity discounts for bulk purchase for sales promotions, premiums, fund-raising, and educational needs. For details, call us at (407) 333-0600 or visit our website at www.charismamedia.com.

To my children, my greatest legacy

My story is for God's glory. He is the One who pursues us and loves us back to life after the unthinkable.

CONTENTS

FOREWORD

YOU MAY HAVE a plan for your life, but sometimes God has a different plan for you. How you cope with that can be the difference between a lifetime of misery and depression and one that is marked by happiness and fulfillment. In this remarkable, touching, and moving memoir, my friends Tracy and Troy Duhon reveal how they had to accept the darkest pain imaginable to be blessed with even greater joy.

I've seen this with so many of the thousands of patients I've worked with over the past thirty-plus years as a psychiatrist and brain health expert at Amen Clinics. In my work I have found that protecting yourself from deep hurts can keep you trapped in anguish. Having the courage to be vulnerable and process the heartache and sorrow can help you turn your pain into purpose. As a Christian, I have seen that with faith comes hope.

Tracy and Troy's story of transformation will make you cry, smile, and even laugh when you least expect it. Their love story is a wild ride that took them in a direction they never anticipated—one that has culminated in a charitable organization that offers hope to orphaned children, helps feed the hungry, and helps house those in need. It's no surprise to me that this fills their hearts with joy. Our brain-imaging work, as well as years of neuroscience research, shows that giving back to others promotes positive changes in the brain that are associated with happiness.

I know this faith-centered couple through their work with my Change Your Brain Foundation, which helps people with mental health issues access the brain imaging and treatment they need within Amen Clinics. Together we are committed to changing people's lives for the better—something that enriches our own lives along the way.

Their inspiring message of hope and healing, which shines through on every page of this book, can help you look at your own life with a fresh perspective to find God's purpose for you. This book is a blessing.

—DANIEL G. AMEN, MD
CEO AND FOUNDER, AMEN CLINICS, BRAINMD,
AND THE CHANGE YOUR BRAIN FOUNDATION

ACKNOWLEDGMENTS

No BOOK IS written in a vacuum. Several people helped make this book possible.

I'd like to thank my husband, Troy, for encouraging me to write my story, and those friends and family members who walked this journey with me. You were the arms that held me up and the light in my darkest moments when I couldn't see.

INTRODUCTION

*Yes, my soul, find rest in God; my
hope comes from him.*

—PSALM 62:5, NIV

THERE ARE TWO things I always knew with absolute certainty: I love God, and I wanted to be a mother.

For as long as I could remember, to become a mother was my greatest hope. Long before I ever set foot in a delivery room—even before I got married—I dreamed of how it would feel to hold my precious babies, how my life would change when they arrived. I saw it as such a beautiful miracle, the gift of motherhood.

I never could have prepared myself for the dark, painful path God would lead me down to realize my heart's desire. My journey was marked by heartbreaking loss and sorrow, but I came out on the other side with a greater sense of purpose and a deeper awareness that God's plan is better than my own, even when it includes suffering.

I lay there, staring at those four sterile walls that felt like an emotional prison. It was the second time I'd found myself in this place. I had just carried another baby to term and delivered him in the presence of family, doctors, and nurses. This was a moment most mothers dream of and cherish long after their delivery experience, but there was no joy for me. I knew I had a limited amount of time with my son and would have to say goodbye—again.

I would leave the hospital empty-handed, no beautiful newborn in my arms to bring home to meet his siblings for the first time. There would be no diapers, no feedings, no milestone moments to record. For the second time in less than three years, I would leave that hospital with only the memory of my son's short life—the fleeting smell of his head, the touch of his fingers, the feel of his skin.

I had buried one son already. I didn't think I could bear having to do so again. The pain in my heart was so excruciating I felt numb. I knew I was being called to trust my Abba Father, but it was so hard. My heart was so broken. I didn't understand why God would allow this to happen to us not once but twice.

Where had I gone so wrong in my life? Where had *we* gone wrong? Why would God allow this to happen? I started to question everything—every decision and choice I had ever made leading up to that moment.

As a mother, I can't imagine any greater pain than losing a child. I was angry and felt a huge hole in my heart. The physical scars of giving birth would heal. The tearstains on my cheeks would eventually fade. But there would always be a missing piece. Our boys were not with us on earth. I could only look to heaven and know they were there as part of God's bigger plan.

In my darkest moments I did the only thing I knew to do—I turned to God and His Word. I chose to trust Him, even when I was full of questions, pain, and anger. The only thing that kept me going was believing that one day God would give me the family I always wanted and write my story just as I had envisioned it.

I would soon learn God had a plan already in motion that was much greater than my own. It wasn't until He helped me crawl out of the darkness and brokenness that I was able to begin to see it and realize I didn't get to control my story. I was simply called to trust the Lord with my whole heart.

Step by step and day by day life began to take shape. The pain of losing our boys didn't go away, but I began to see that while our children were not with us here on earth, their memory would live on through the mosaic God was crafting from all the broken pieces of our hearts.

Allowing God to work in my life created a space for Him to turn my greatest pain into my life's greatest purpose. I noticed the injustices happening around me. I began to see hurting people, and I wanted to meet them exactly where they were in their time of need. I learned how to love extravagantly and give in a way I didn't know I was capable of until I had gone through my own suffering. Only God could have birthed that kind of love in me. After the pain I had experienced, I began to see the world through God's eyes rather than my own.

I thought losing my boys would be the end of life as I knew it. It was, in a way. My dream of motherhood took a very different form, but I came to know the joy and beauty of being able to change the lives of children, my own and so many others. I would get my miracle.

God is the master storyteller, and this is the story He wrote for me. It is my family's story and the story of Giving Hope, the ministry born from our experience. But this is also *your* story. I hope this book will inspire you to look beyond your own pain, stop running from mistakes, and realize God loves you and can use you through any situation. When you truly learn to embrace our heavenly Father's unconditional love, you can change your heart, your life, and the world.

Our story is told mostly from my point of view, but at times you'll hear from my husband, Troy. We processed our pain differently, but by the grace of God our losses didn't drive us apart. Instead, they brought us together to serve in a way we never dreamed. Today we are raising money to help families adopt, building Hope Homes to care for orphaned children around the world, operating a food pantry and community center in New Orleans, and much more. Through all the pain and tears, we held on to hope, and God has brought so much beauty out of our heartbreak.

I wish we could be sitting together, sipping our favorite drinks and talking face to face. While I can't be with you personally, I have placed QR codes throughout this book that will direct you to bonus videos I recorded just for you. These videos are designed to be viewed at the start of each chapter. You can use a smartphone to access this content, or you can visit tracyduhon.com/videos or scan the QR code below and click on the links to view the same bonus material. You'll find the first video at the end of this introduction.

Let's Talk

tracyduhon.com/videos

I know you have your own story, your own pain. Everything I've learned has been by taking one painful step after another. When I didn't know which way was up, my goal was simply to move forward. Sometimes it felt as if I were inching along, but now I look back on our journey and marvel at what God has done.

If you remember nothing else from this book, I hope you remember this: God can bring purpose out of your pain too. That is what our story is about—it is about looking back on the moments we didn't think we could survive but did. It is about finding our purpose in the depths of our suffering. It is about having unwavering faith, trusting God, and holding on to hope even through the unthinkable.

With God there is always hope.

When we're in the midst of our greatest pain, sometimes hope is all we have.

Let's Talk

tracyduhon.com/videos/introduction

Chapter 1

GOD'S TIMING

"For I know the plans I have for you," declares
the LORD, "plans to prosper you and not to harm
you, plans to give you hope and a future."
—JEREMIAH **29:11**, NIV

tracyduhon.com/videos/ch1

WHEN I LOOK back on my life, I see the moments so clearly—the rays of light beaming through the sky, guiding the way and reminding me over and over that God is with me. Through the peaks and valleys and even in the storms, He has been there. Always.

We never know what we might find ourselves navigating in life, and we must remember to hold steadfast in our faith through those highs and lows. When I think of my family's valleys, I remember the times when I had only my faith to lean on. Without God I never would have made it through any of it. Our family wouldn't be where we are today. The pain we endured serves as a reminder to remain humble when we are gazing out from the highest peaks and give glory to God, for only He could have brought us this far.

God uses broken people to carry His message into the world. We see it in the Scriptures, and I've seen it in my own life. God brought us through brokenness and restored both my heart and our family in a way that has empowered us to serve people across the globe.

Two decades ago I never could have imagined any of it.

I think back to when Troy and I were a young couple learning how to navigate all the normal challenges in marriage. We had no idea the devastating loss we would face or that the pain would give us a greater purpose and change the direction of our lives.

Losing a child is unimaginable. Yet it ignited me in ways that to this day leave me speechless at times. I've poured that passion not only into our family but into the work we are doing here in the United States and around the world.

Giving Hope, the ministry Troy and I founded, was birthed from a deep desire to love others well and meet people exactly where they are. Our heart is to promote human dignity by serving the most vulnerable among us and ultimately give glory to God.

It is our sons' legacy in action.

After losing my two boys, Jonathon and Joseph, I felt the heart of our heavenly Father. As I walked through my own pain and grief,

I had to let go of the baggage that was preventing me from living God's plan to the fullest.

I began to connect with others who were also experiencing loss. After everything that happened, I have devoted myself to my family and this mission.

God carried us through, but it wasn't until I realized there were parts of the journey that we still needed to walk out that we all began to heal. For so long I ran from that walk. I walked solely in the Lord when what I needed to do was also process the losses—*really* process.

Staying busy could only get me so far. In addition to

being steadfast in faith, there was work I needed to do so I could be exactly who God created me to be. There were still places I needed to heal. I had to step into the pain, so I prayed, studied the Word, worshipped, and sought counsel. Through my healing process I truly began to see God's purpose for my life. I had to let go of the baggage that was preventing me from living God's plan to the fullest.

What are you holding on to that is preventing you from truly living out God's plan for your life? I have realized through my own experience that we are all holding on to something. That something will often make us feel safely hidden behind our pain or shame, but it is the very thing God wants us to give to Him.

When we lost the boys, I wanted to believe that if I did enough, it would fix everything, that I could shield my family from the pain. I did the best I knew to do at that time. I wanted to protect the people I love from the things in this world that are painful. But my attempts to protect myself and my family were actually hurting us.

Now, all these years later, I see that as we have poured into Giving Hope, not only has God given our family an opportunity to help others, but He has healed our broken pieces in the process. This is part of the beauty God brings out of ashes, the good He works together through our trials. He uses each of us in different ways, and by helping others, we continue to heal ourselves.

Our family lost a piece of our hearts that can never be replaced. We feel that loss in some way or another almost every day. Loss isn't something that just goes away. Some days are better than others. It changes as the years pass, but it is always there.

It has been nineteen years since our Jonathon took his last breath and we said goodbye as he was promoted to heaven. That was the first time my heart broke. The second time was two years later when we lost Joseph.

By helping others, we continue to heal ourselves.

As I cried in the months after Joseph left us, God spoke to my heart: "Daughter, I will take the pain away, but you have to give it to Me!"

In letting go and giving it all to God, our story began to unfold. Our pain was met with purpose. Our hearts were filled with a hope that only God can give.

That hope would eventually lead us halfway around the world.

LISTENING TO GOD'S VOICE

It was October 15, 2012. We were in China at a government office with many other couples.

It was Gotcha Day.

As I stood there excited to meet our daughter for the first time, I couldn't help but think about everything that had led to that moment. Troy and I were on the other side of the world, had a new baby at home with our two oldest children, and had two boys in heaven.

The trip to Beijing had been planned for months. When we learned the adoption had gone through after seven years of praying and waiting, my greatest hope was for her to bond with us and feel secure. I spent weeks leading up to the trip sending photos and recordings of books we had read so she could get used to our voices. We mailed boxes of other items that would make our first meeting feel familiar so she would know we were her family.

The moment God put adoption on my heart in 2005, He destined me to be this child's mother. We had prayed for years for the little girl we would be welcoming into our family. I wanted her to feel that love even before we held her for the first time. I wanted her to know she would have a forever home centered in the Lord and surrounded by love, and that God had hand-picked us to all be a family.

Our pain was met with purpose.

Our precious girl was being torn from the only home she had known at the very young age of eleven months. So I prayed endlessly for her little heart to be comforted with the love of God.

All the preparation, all the prayers—it felt as if it had

taken so long for this moment to come, and now here we were, about to meet her.

I was overcome with emotion, thinking about everything along the way that had happened—the journey, the loss, the pain, the darkness—and then I thought about the joy, hope, faith, trust, and power of redemption. The last several years of our lives were coming full circle as we stood thousands of miles away in a foreign country about to meet our daughter.

Our guide that day was an absolute godsend. I wanted to know where our beautiful baby girl came from, and our guide walked us through her story and helped us understand. I had never been to China, but I wanted to know everything so I could help my daughter write her story. I wanted her to understand her origin, her culture, where her life began despite where she might find herself as part of our family. The guide was our first connection with the world where our daughter's life began.

We had decided to take the five-hour drive from the government office to tour the orphanage where she had been living. I thought it would help us learn more about our daughter's life. I had never set foot inside an orphanage, but because this was the only home she had known, I felt I needed to. I prayed that God would allow me to truly "see" her and provide for her in a way this place couldn't or hadn't. The tour was necessary for that reason.

I was not prepared for what I saw, and it broke my heart.

We walked in and were greeted by the staff. There were photos of children all over the wall. They showed us their daily routine. I know they did their best to clean before our visit and present a positive image, but I did not see happy children. The sights and smells—they were sobering.

In one of the rooms, we saw a collection of little playpens reminiscent of dog pens all lined up together filling the space. As I walked by the playpens, I couldn't help but lay my hand on each child. Many had special needs. I knew there were still two more floors beyond this one with more children; with each step it was as though the crack in my heart grew.

At one point I saw a few older girls and envisioned what my daughter's life would have been like if she had stayed there. I just wanted to get her home to start her new life.

After the tour we went back to the government office and watched as children came out one by one to meet their adoptive parents. Some were older; some were younger. Many came out crying as they were leaving the only caregiver they had ever known and being turned over to complete strangers. I was nervous, praying constantly that God would connect our hearts with our daughter's the moment we saw one another.

She came out last, carried by one of the women

because she was still so little. I don't think Troy and I were prepared for the emotion that swallowed us whole when they put her in our arms. I was holding a piece of heaven. God planned all this. After all we had experienced—losing two babies just hours after their birth—it was so incredible to be holding this beautiful little girl.

She didn't cry. I held her and called her name. She held my face and touched my hair. She knew. We were family. Maybe it was the photos and boxes of items we had sent, but there was a peace in the moment that made it feel divine.

As the caregivers took a photo of us, I was so thankful to be taking her out of that orphanage. I couldn't help but be painfully aware that she was one of the only children without special needs. My heart was breaking. I couldn't stop crying.

I closed my eyes and prayed, "What are You saying, Lord? Why did You bring me here?"

He needed to break my heart a little more for me to see clearly.

When I imagined this day, I envisioned a celebration. The tears were a sign that God was stirring something within me, and I knew I needed to listen. I felt helpless and kept wondering, "What about the rest of these children?" I wanted to take them all home, but I knew that wasn't possible.

I wanted to follow where the Lord was leading me, but He needed to break my heart a little more for me to see clearly. It was as if the crack that had begun in my heart during the tour had burst open, and I was standing there shattered and wanting to help.

I couldn't let it go. I had my baby girl, but it wasn't enough. I knew there were so many other children in need. I kept asking Troy, "What can we do?" But for the longest time, we had no answers, so I prayed and turned the question over to God.

Have you ever been deeply pained by the injustices in the world and wondered if God was trying to tell you something? Have you felt a stirring within, a longing to make an impact, something drawing you to help? We are all called to *something* that ignites us in ways we know can only be the work of God, but it sometimes takes monumental moments for us to realize it.

The time in China had gripped me. I didn't know what would happen next, but the seed had been planted. It wouldn't be until we were back in the comfort of our lives, halfway across the world, that the seed would begin to take form and grow into something more. So much more.

Chapter 2

TRUST

Trust in the Lord completely, and do not rely on your own opinions. With all your heart rely on him to guide you, and he will lead you in every decision you make.

—PROVERBS 3:5, TPT

tracyduhon.com/videos/ch2

For you to truly understand our story and all that God has done in our lives, we need to start at the beginning.

I grew up in Marrero, Louisiana, on the West Bank of New Orleans, the daughter of a fisherman. My mother was a city girl. She and my father met on a blind date; fifty-nine years later they are still together. My upbringing was simple, and of all the things my parents taught me, the most important were love and faith.

Like many people, I struggled as a young woman to truly understand self-confidence and feel secure in who I was. I grew up thinking I had to be and act a certain way. I thought my life had to follow a certain prescription. It took me until around the age of twenty-seven to finally break free of those misconceptions and truly embrace the woman God made me to be. It wasn't easy, and I made mistakes along the way, mistakes that later in life I would think might be the reason I went through so much pain.

God is a God of love. He is our Father and Redeemer. He loves us through all our choices, good or bad.

I had to work through the guilt and shame of my past mistakes and remind myself that God is a God of love. He is our Father and Redeemer. He loves us through all our choices, good or bad. With each choice, we get the opportunity to learn from it, grow closer to Him, and become a better version of ourselves. With each decision to accept His love and follow His way, we grow into the person He created us to be.

My mother, Gail, was truly amazing. I learned so much from her, and I now share those lessons with my own daughters. She is a woman of prayer and has spent countless hours praying for and with me. She taught me that we grow through disappointment and that we must love people with the love of God regardless of where they are. This is really the fabric of who I am, and it started with her. My mother's love carried me through times when I was still learning to forgive myself. She was a daily example of what it looks like to have an intimate relationship with Jesus Christ.

Like many families, mine had a healthy dose of dysfunction. My mother and father worked very hard when I was a young girl. Because my dad was a fisherman, he was offshore for weeks at a time. My mom took great care of us but wanted my father to be home more. I remember being afraid of my dad because he was very strict and would get angry. I was the middle child and a challenge for my parents because I wanted to do things my own way.

We were a close family, but we had many financial challenges when my dad was off trawling on the bayou. The winter months were particularly difficult. My mom began to work as a night auditor at a hotel, and my dad would work two jobs just to make ends meet. We also experienced bankruptcy and lost the home my parents worked so hard to build.

My mother was a devout Catholic but didn't always go to church when I was young. My dad was not really into church. But one day my mom began attending church again, and it changed everything for her and our family. She recommitted her life to the Lord, and my father followed.

My parents accepted Christ when I was eleven years old, which was around the same time I finally started to open myself up a bit more to new experiences. Up to that point, I was very insecure and overly dependent on my mother. I hated school. I love learning now, but school wasn't easy for me, and back then I wanted no part of it.

I was a little girl who loved God. I didn't know Him personally, but I knew He existed, and I loved Him and longed to grow my faith in Him. God was a place of comfort and peace for me.

As a teenager I attended a Christian school. I loved it and learned so much spiritually, but in terms of my education, it was not great. I was there from ages fourteen to sixteen, and then when I was seventeen, my parents decided to move to Oklahoma City. While my older sister and younger brother planned to go with them, I wanted to stay in New Orleans, but I was only seventeen and didn't know how to earn a living. So I did the only thing I knew to do to feel safe and secure: I got married.

We all got married young back then. It was just what we did. He and I didn't even date. We went to school together, and I liked him, but I did not truly understand what marriage was about or the value of a covenant marriage. I didn't even pray or ask God to show me if this was His plan for my life. I just did it. I was a Christian and thought I knew what I was doing. Everyone else was getting married, so I thought I was supposed to do that too. I was married for a year before we divorced. I married again at age nineteen and was divorced by twenty.

Just writing those last two sentences breaks my heart. For many years I felt I had failed God by breaking the covenant of marriage. I made those decisions because I thought I had to marry the person I dated. It was a combination of my upbringing and lack of understanding of what dating is supposed to look like. I was young and immature in this area of my life, and I was clearly doing my own thing. I didn't realize the choices I was making then were life-changing.

I was always rebellious and did the opposite of what I was told to do, but it took me a long time to make peace with those two choices to marry. The culmination of those three years of my life was the tipping point for me to realize that I needed to accept that I had made those mistakes and move on. I had to allow myself to be free. My mom once said to me, "Jesus forgave you. Now you must forgive yourself." I worked hard to do just that, but it wasn't easy.

I was broken and alone, far from my family. The guilt and shame I felt for being twice divorced was excruciating. I hurt my family, myself, and others. My mom told me God removes our sin as far as the east is from the west. Still, it was a challenge for me to take those first steps toward forgiving myself and receiving God's forgiveness. I had this idea that God wanted me to be a good girl, and now I felt I had failed Him.

> I did the only thing I knew to do to feel safe and secure: I got married.

This was a tough season in my life. I went from a hopeful seventeen-year-old with big dreams to a sad twenty-year-old with broken dreams. I spent the next year and a half taking one step at a time and working on myself. I started going to church again, studying the Bible, praying, and connecting with a mature community of people who were willing to walk alongside me. I had two jobs to earn enough money to provide for myself, and I began to grow in my relationship with Christ. This was the beginning of me seeing the love of God at work in my life. I was finally able to feel

His forgiveness. I believed He loved and forgave me, and I was finally able to let go of the guilt I had been holding on to.

I met Troy a year later.

TURNING TO GOD

I would love to tell you we had a fairy-tale love story, but that just isn't true—at least it wasn't at first. It became more of a fairy-tale romance later in our relationship, after we learned and grew and put the work in. We're still working at it.

Troy and I were crazy about each other, but we were also driving each other crazy. Our lives were consumed with partying, and we were both abusing drugs and alcohol. It was a rough season for us individually and as a couple. Our lifestyle was a recipe for disaster. To say God wasn't at the center of our relationship is an understatement. Our life together back then looked nothing like it does now.

I had never met anyone like Troy. He captured my heart. He was confident and successful as the general sales manager of a thriving car dealership. A lot of people were interested in him for what he had or what he could do as opposed to who he was as a person. But I just loved Troy, despite our crazy lifestyle and all the ways we were unintentionally hurting each other. I knew he had an amazing heart. It was the thing he loved most about me—that I saw him.

WHEN HOPE IS ALL YOU HAVE

We were living in the fast lane and nearly broke up several times, but we loved each other, and that is what kept us together during those wild days. In my heart I knew something had to change. This wasn't how we were supposed to be living our lives, and I knew if we continued down this path, I would end up empty, or worse, dead.

One day after a rough weekend of partying, Troy and I had our usual upsets and were both feeling empty. I decided to get on my knees in prayer and call out to the One who had rescued me before. I believed He would somehow help again. As I prayed, I knew things would begin to change, but it took me doing my part.

I started going to church again, and I was praying every day for God to guide us out of the world we'd found ourselves engulfed in. That season was hard and nearly broke me. I considered leaving Troy and prayed that if I wasn't supposed to be with him, God would remove him from my life. This was the first time I asked God to help me in a relationship. When God didn't remove him, I knew I needed to do something. Troy was meant to be in my life but not like this. Something needed to change.

I turned my life over completely to the Lord. I began to seek the Jesus my mother believed in and served. I started attending a Bible study with my friend Cathy. In less than six months, Troy saw the changes in me and followed. We started attending a church together, and there we were loved, supported, and encouraged as a couple. The year before we got married, Troy was baptized.

When we talk to couples and friends about those early days, we often say that Troy pulled me into the wild world of drugs and alcohol, and when I turned to faith, I pulled him out of it. I returned to my roots, knowing my mother's prayers for me were being answered. The process of leaving our partying world to follow Jesus wasn't easy, but it changed the entire course of our relationship and set a new direction for our future family. I grabbed hold of the Word of God and let it take root deep within me. It became my foundation.

When all hell broke loose, I chose God, and it is what shifted me from a weak, insecure woman to a strong, secure one. I found my confidence. Christ was living in me, and I found my strength in Him. My transformation became the catalyst that turned both of our lives around.

THE POWER OF PRAYER

Like me, Troy came from a family of faith. In fact, he was a preacher's kid. Both of us had been given a good foundation. Faith was ingrained in us. We just didn't know how to build on it together. As we grew up, we found other pursuits and forgot some of those early lessons we learned at home. Like many others, we ultimately had to realize for ourselves that we needed to turn back to God.

Troy and I were always loving and generous people, even in the wild days, but we were building on the wrong foundation. We needed God at the center of our lives. Getting there wasn't easy, but our story serves as a reminder that no one is too far out of reach for God.

Our first year of marriage was difficult. There were days when it felt more like it was him against me than us against the world. There wasn't an *us*. We hadn't found a rhythm where we were working together. Troy was being investigated for something that had happened in the business, and I was trying to create a beautiful home. We were both focusing on what we needed and wanted as individuals.

I knew Troy had a big heart and the capacity to love and give extravagantly, but he was very independent, and it took some effort for us to start working together as a couple. The blessing during this time was that although Troy was facing a difficult situation at work, for the first time, he truly felt protected and covered by God. It was that realization that allowed us to break down some of the walls keeping us from working together.

No one is too far out of reach for God.

We were attending Bible studies and beginning to build our relationship with Christ in the center. We were being intentional, but there were still roadblocks along the way. What I came to realize about my husband is that while his independence got him what he desired in business, it was holding us back as a couple.

That is not to say I didn't bring my issues into the marriage as well. I had an expectation of how our marriage should be and the role Troy should be playing in that vision. I was giving my all, but it didn't feel like a two-way street. We seemed to be on two different paths, with me trying to make our house into a home and Troy focused on his work.

Like any couple, those first years of marriage were a learning process for both of us. Couples sometimes have this idea that once the vows are exchanged, they will just magically form a beautiful union. That couldn't be further from the truth. Even if two people love each other dearly, until they learn to work together; honor the fact that they each have their own ideas, needs, and goals; and *work* to understand their partner, their marriage will be an uphill battle.

Troy and I needed to learn how to compromise and merge our lives together. But that wasn't the only thing that would make a difference for us. I once heard it said that couples who pray together stay together. That is a solid truth Troy and I have come to know in our marriage.

During those early years, I learned to pray for my husband. I picked up Stormie Omartian's book *The Power of a Praying Wife*, and her testimony of how prayer changed her own marriage gave me hope and taught me how to pray for Troy. I began to pray for him every single day. Sometimes I would pray the prayers she suggested, and other times I would ask the Holy Spirit to show me what Troy needed. I saw the power of prayer firsthand in my marriage. I wasn't leaving my marriage up to chance; I knew only God could make Troy into the man he was created to be. I was simply a vessel. I came to see that prayer was the answer for everything.

Prayer cannot be our last resort; it must be our first response.

Troy and I had to learn to face ourselves—both our strengths and the things holding us back. We had to learn to give *and* receive. We had to learn that when we had disagreements or just weren't on the same page about something, we needed to actively seek God and understanding as opposed to holding on to resentment and hurt feelings. It was a learning process we needed to navigate through as a couple. But looking back, I see that God used the challenges in our early days together to prepare us for the struggles we would endure years down the road.

Even to this day, Troy and I continue to invest our

time and money into improving our marriage. We know this is key to creating the life we want, not only as a couple but for our family.

I have always been a fighter, but fighting for Troy and our marriage is what led me to turn my life back over to God and fully surrender my plans and heart to Him. For the first time, I trusted God to lead my life, and that trust helped me gain the strength I needed then and would need even more later.

Surrendering our lives to the Lord and taking steps to change the way we were living gave God room to work in us. It wasn't easy. We had to be very intentional, but doing so led us to a place where we learned to forgive and incorporate prayer into every aspect of our lives.

Without Troy there would be no story. My marriage coach, Barb, once said Troy helped make me the woman I am today, and she is right. We have done that for each other. God breathed life into us and our relationship. When we turned to Him and chose to trust Him fully, our lives changed.

I live in awe each day as I bear witness to what God can do in a person's life, marriage, and family. I have seen the miracles, both great and small, that come through prayer.

If we want to see God transform our lives in any way—whether the issue is with our marriage, children, family, or career—prayer cannot be our last resort; it must be our first response.

Chapter 3

FAITHFUL

Trust in the LORD *and do good; dwell in the land and cultivate faithfulness. Delight yourself in the* LORD*; and He will give you the desires of your heart. Commit your way to the* LORD*, trust also in Him, and He will do it.*

—PSALM 37:3–5

tracyduhon.com/videos/ch3

TROY AND I were married in 1995 and lived on Paris Avenue. Those years were a beautiful mess of growing and learning together. I once heard someone say some gardens take a long time to flourish, and that certainly was the case with us. We did a lot of things wrong, but I believe the thread of our love for each other and the Lord ultimately created this happy place for us.

I was full of hope for the future. Finally, at around the age of twenty-seven, I felt comfortable in my own skin. I knew who I was; I was strong in my faith. Troy and I continued to work together to build our marriage each day. Then I became a mother at age twenty-nine. It was a dream come true, the greatest gift. The plan we had for our life was coming together. Troy and I had been together for six years and married for almost two. We were ready to start our family.

When I first learned I was pregnant, I was so excited. It was the greatest thing I could imagine. I probably took four pregnancy tests, just to make sure. I have heard other women say they did the same thing, that they didn't believe the first test, so they took several more. Believe it or not, I saved all the tests and now have them as keepsakes.

I was still working at the time and was going in to the doctor for routine checkups. At one point I started to have some challenges with the pregnancy and was in pain. At the time, my doctor was out of town, and I was told I was likely having a tubal pregnancy.

That news really began my journey of learning how to have faith for my children even before they were born. I was praying, "Lord, make me a mama." It didn't matter that the baby hadn't been born yet; I was mothering my child already. From the minute you see two lines or read the word *pregnant* on the test, start to mother that baby, and don't allow fear to take hold. That's what I did up to the moment the doctors finally confirmed that everything was OK—and that's what I continued to do.

I loved being pregnant and knowing I was carrying a little life inside me. I had so many emotions and thoughts about how I would care for this child and what it would be like to be a mother. I read everything I could to prepare to be the best mom I could be. I was working, eating normally, and generally enjoying my pregnancy. I had some premature contractions around six months, but for the most part it was an amazing pregnancy.

God knows best and would give me exactly what I needed.

Both Troy and I had so much anticipation during those months. We didn't want to find out the gender of the baby because that made the experience even more exciting for us. It was such a beautiful time in our lives.

As a first-time mom, I didn't know what I would or wouldn't need, so I bought *everything*. The baby's room was white, and I had a mural painted on the wall of a little boy and girl holding a lamb. It was stunning. Years later it would speak vividly to what we would walk through, showing the little boy and girl I dreamed of having and Jesus, the Lamb, walking with us. It would prove to be a prophetic piece of art, but at the time, I just thought it was beautiful, and it spoke to me.

I didn't care whether I was having a boy or girl. I was so in love with that baby. I trusted that God knows best and would give me exactly what I needed.

THE ARRIVAL

Toward the end of my pregnancy, I was working short days. I was doing hair at the time and could manage to put in only around three hours per day three days a week. I still loved being pregnant; I felt great and looked cute. It was just getting more and more difficult to be on my feet for long periods of time.

On my last day of work my back started hurting. I went home and ordered a huge pizza and sat on the sofa to eat it. I think back and have to laugh because I just don't eat like that—ever. But when I was pregnant, I loved it. I would order roast beef po'boy sandwiches and nachos, stuff I would never eat now. But during that first pregnancy I couldn't get enough.

As I sat on the sofa, the back pain intensified. Because I didn't really know what to expect, I didn't immediately realize I was having contractions. It was the most incredible pain. I was on the phone with a friend who kept telling me she thought I was having back labor. This went on for four hours. Eventually we hung up the phone, and she headed to my house.

It was go time.

When she arrived, I had to crawl to the door to let her in—that's how bad the pain was. It's something you never forget. I called Troy, and he was going to meet us at the hospital. I had grabbed my water and my makeup bag. I was not leaving the house without *either*, but if one took priority, it was my makeup bag. That was just me then.

When we arrived at the hospital, I was four centimeters dilated. My doctor wasn't on call, and instead, a doctor walked in and said it looked as if the baby was much bigger than six pounds and delivering vaginally could be difficult.

The contractions had been going on for about ten hours at that point. She let me go a little longer, opting to monitor the situation. I was given an epidural, and as it kicked in, my boom box was playing worship music. We were having church up in that room. Let's have this baby!

Still convinced a vaginal delivery could be complicated, the doctor ultimately decided to perform a C-section. All my kids love drama. This was just the beginning.

I went into the operating room, with Troy and my mother right there with me, and gave birth to an eight-pound, five-ounce, twenty-one-inch baby boy. He was crying, but when I called him by his name, he calmed down. They put him by my face, and my heart just melted. That dark curly hair, my boy—I just loved him so much.

He is the only one of our children Troy named: Joshua Joseph. Joshua is also the only one of my children I got to experience labor with. There were a lot of firsts with him. God knew exactly what He was doing by blessing us with our son first.

Each of my children grew my faith in different ways and helped me grow into the mother I am.

I love all my children the same, but there is a tenderness with Joshua because everything we experienced together was the first. He made me a mother and a more faithful daughter of God. I became an even more prayerful woman.

I adore all my children and pray for them every day, but the bond Joshua and I share is beautiful. We are truly joined at the hip and the heart. Troy was working a lot during that time, so I did almost everything with Joshua and took him nearly everywhere I went. There were so many moments when it was just the two of us. It was such a special time.

With Troy's full support, I decided to stop working once Joshua was born and just poured myself into being his mother. Twenty-six years later I still absolutely love being his mom.

When Troy and I talked about growing our family, we had always planned to have children three years apart. It was all coming together. I spent three years and one month with Joshua before our little bundle of joy Abigail Cheramie was born.

FINDING JOY

I thought I was pregnant again. After going through it once before, I just knew. I did all the same things to confirm, again taking multiple tests, which I also saved. I was thirty-two years old at the time. Once again, we decided not to find out the gender, so we had the same level of anticipation and excitement that we did before.

When I was pregnant with Joshua, I had purchased two baby outfits for the hospital, one for a boy and one for a girl. Because friends and family didn't know the gender either, we received gifts for both boys and girls. We had saved the items from those who fell into the girl camp and figured whether baby two was a boy or a girl, we were ready!

That pregnancy was another faith journey. Looking back, I realize each of my children grew my faith in different ways and helped me grow into the mother I am. I wouldn't trade one bit of it, even the worst parts.

With Abigail, I ended up having premature contractions. I was told I had partial placenta previa when I was about seven months along. That meant part of my cervix was blocked, which can cause bleeding. We had planned a trip to Disney World with friends, but because of these health concerns I needed to get the doctor's clearance. Sure enough, I got the clearance. My mother didn't think I should travel, but I wanted to go on that trip. It was Josh's first time at Disney World, and I wasn't going to miss it.

God showed up in my room that night. I felt His peace that surpasses all understanding.

From the moment we landed, the trip was anything but what we had planned. I started bleeding and ended up in the hospital for five days. Troy decided to have our dear friends take Josh home and spent the night getting him ready to fly while I was at the hospital by myself.

That night became a defining moment for me. I was afraid I might lose the baby because the bleeding was so severe. I was not able to get out of bed and was being given medication via an IV to help stop the contractions. I prayed all night. It was still too early to deliver. I turned on the Christian radio station to help myself stay calm, and God showed up in my room that night. I felt His peace that surpasses all understanding.

In a hospital room far from home, my husband, and my baby boy, I was up in the wee hours of the morning, praying over my baby, mothering her just as I had Joshua when the doctors thought he was a tubal pregnancy. In those tense hours when I thought we might lose her, my Abba Father imparted to me a faith that would carry me through the entire journey.

The bleeding was a result of the partial previa. The baby was OK, but it was still very scary. The doctors needed to get me stable before they could discharge me. Those days were long, and it felt like an eternity before I was finally back in the comfort of our home.

I was on bed rest after I returned. Then, three weeks before my due date, I delivered Abigail via C-section at the doctor's recommendation. She was eight pounds, thirteen ounces, this beautiful baby girl whom I had hoped and prayed for. My son stole my heart, and when my daughter was born, I felt so fulfilled. I always wanted a little girl, and we now had our princess.

My mom and Troy's mom, Meme, were in the delivery room with me and Troy, and the entire hospital could hear us screaming when Abigail arrived.

We were so excited to have this beautiful little girl to love. She looked just like my sister and was the happiest baby, joyfully waving her arms and kicking her legs, the epitome of her name.

Joshua means *warrior*, and Abigail means *joy*. They both live up to those names.

LIVING THE DREAM

Our family was growing, and it was amazing. I was having the most incredible time being Troy's wife and the mother of our children. Joshua just loved his little sister. With the four of us together, it felt as if so many prayers had been answered.

When Josh turned three, I started to homeschool. I loved it. The kids and I were inseparable. I had fun with the kids while also caring for them. It was hard and a lot of work. There were lots of sleepless nights, dirty dishes, and dirty diapers, and it was all made more challenging by the need to also nurture our marriage. But I was thankful I could commit that time to them and be there for them in that way. Life wasn't without stress, but my heart was so happy.

Even looking back on it now, while there were a lot of growing pains, there was so much joy. It really was the best of times. I loved my life, and my prayer was simple: I wanted to have more children and continue growing our family.

Chapter 4

LOSS

But he answered me, "My grace is always more than enough for you, and my power finds its full expression through your weakness." So I will celebrate my weaknesses, for when I'm weak I sense more deeply the mighty power of Christ living in me.

—2 CORINTHIANS 12:9, TPT

Let's Talk

tracyduhon.com/videos/ch4

I PLANNED TO HAVE a baby every three years, and the plan was coming together just as I had hoped. I was continuing to draw closer to the Lord, and I felt fulfilled.

From the outside looking in, we had everything: our businesses were doing well, we had a beautiful home, and we were growing a family that loved God and one another. We were so blessed. Troy and I still had a lot of growing to do in our marriage, but as we continued to work together, we built a deeper level of trust between us.

Major shifts were happening in our lives. Troy was trusting me and my counsel as a wife more and more. He got a life coach and a pastoral coach to help him grow spiritually and professionally. We were buying more car dealerships and living in the benefit of that success, but I remember his coach telling him, "When I hear you talk about cars, it's what you do. When I hear you talk about God, family, and helping people, you come alive."

Those words really resonated with Troy—with both of us. It was because of that coach that I began to really understand my husband's heart. I felt as though I finally knew how to be his partner. I realized he was a kingdom-minded man and that our job was to help, empower, and raise up. We still didn't know exactly what that would look like, but we recognized the passion was there.

When I found out I was pregnant again, it was exactly on schedule. I wanted to have at least four children. We were on baby number three, and it had been three years since Abigail was born, just as I had planned. I was just as excited seeing the positive pregnancy test result as I had been with the first two. There was something beautiful about realizing a person was growing inside me. With each of my children I began to mother them from the moment I found out I was pregnant.

But this pregnancy wasn't like the others. I lost the baby.

When my stomach started cramping and I began bleeding, I never thought the result would be a miscarriage. I had no idea that was only the beginning of the grief I would experience over the next four years.

I remember lying on the sofa, still bleeding and devastated. I don't remember the pain, but I remember the deep sense of loss I felt. I was seven weeks into the pregnancy and already in love and ready to welcome this baby into our family. This was not supposed to be the next step in our journey.

A New Reality

Loss was foreign to us, and we had no idea how to process it. My heart was to be a wife and mother, and when I was pregnant, I felt close to the Lord, as if everything was as it should be. Things began to change after the miscarriage. I felt the bottom buckling beneath me, and my world began to fall apart. My heart was broken, and my faith was being challenged in a way it hadn't been before. Little did I know, this was just the beginning.

At the time, I just said, "OK, God." I stopped planning. I decided to surrender to God's will for my life and just live.

For many people who have suffered deep loss, the experience becomes a defining moment, the line marking when everything changed. Life is divided into what happened before and what happened after. The miscarriage represented that for us. That loss reminded me that I am not in control and pushed me closer to God as I was forced to face the things I still wanted to control.

I eventually realized I had to *really* turn everything over to Him. It wasn't enough just to say, "OK, God. I surrender." I had to walk out that surrender day by day, sometimes minute by minute.

MOVING FORWARD

There's never a right time to try again. I was pregnant again within a few months. Joshua and Abigail were both healthy, and I chose to believe that this baby would be my redemption after the miscarriage. I was tenacious and persistent; nothing was going to happen to this baby. There was no way. God just wouldn't allow it. The idea that this baby would not be healthy was never even on my radar.

The thing I realized following the miscarriage is my heart would never forget. The child we lost will always be part of me, and so will the memory of that heartache.

I have heard others talk about pregnancy after miscarriage, the rainbow baby. The milestone moments are met with held breath; you celebrate cautiously because you have a new understanding of the fragility of the situation. When we crossed the seven-week mark, I just knew everything was going to be OK. With each week that passed, I stopped holding my breath, and I eventually felt free again.

Around the three-month mark I was scheduled for a routine ultrasound, and the doctors wanted to also do blood work. It was all standard. After Abigail was born, I started having some health issues. None were overly concerning to me. I was dealing with a combination of hypoglycemia, low iron, thyroid issues, and an autoimmune disorder, but I actually felt great.

I was trusting God with my health and the baby's. And those first three months were incredible. Everything looked good. I felt good. The pregnancy was normal.

THE MOMENT

I was waiting calmly when the nurse came in following the ultrasound. From the moment she entered the room, I could see something was wrong. It was written all over her face. She said they were unable to find the baby's kidneys, lungs, or bladder, and there was no amniotic fluid.

You could cut the tension with a knife; the atmosphere was so heavy. My doctor at the time delivered the news quickly and without sugarcoating anything: "This baby is going to die inside you." He advised me to abort the pregnancy.

I didn't know what to think, how to feel, or even how to process what I had been told. I convinced myself the ultrasound was wrong, that the machine must have malfunctioned. I needed him to be wrong. I needed all this to be a misunderstanding. It had to be a mistake.

We would have to wait another four weeks for the next ultrasound to confirm the baby's condition. I believed with everything in me that God wouldn't allow this baby to die. I held on to that hope during those weeks. I also knew I couldn't keep that doctor. I was destroyed by the news, and hearing it week after week was unbearable. I needed a doctor who would walk

At twenty weeks the worst was confirmed.

through this *with* me. I still didn't believe the doctor's report was true, but I wanted someone to have faith with me, even for the impossible.

I had heard of Dr. Bennie Nobles. He was in high demand, as he specialized in high-risk pregnancies. I also knew he was a godly, faith-filled man. He was the person I needed to walk through this with me. I knew he would approach this with both the faith and the medical expertise needed in this situation. I just knew he was my doctor.

I went to see him when I was around nineteen weeks pregnant. His associate saw me that day, as Dr. Bennie was traveling. He validated what we had previously been told: the baby did not have kidneys or a bladder.

At twenty weeks the worst was confirmed.

The news was devastating, but I still walked out of there with hope. Dr. Kennedy didn't make me feel as if all was lost. A week later I still had hope. Dr. Bennie never told me the baby would live, but I felt cared for when we discussed the prognosis. That care helped me hold on to hope through the absolute worst.

Despite being hopeful, I was still dealing with a lot of anger. I just couldn't believe this was happening. I needed the Lord to walk me through this and help me understand.

My family was around me, and I clung to them because other than my faith, they were the only thing keeping me going. I felt so devastated that at times,

I couldn't even mother the children I already had. I wanted to love on Josh and Abigail and be the mother they needed me to be, but it was so hard. I was trying to hold on to hope, but I was hurt, angry, and crushed emotionally.

We were getting weekly checkups with the specialist and ultrasounds every three weeks. I was on bed rest and would sit in the midnight hour, praying and asking for this baby's organs to grow. I would cry, often sobbing myself to sleep. I prayed over him and for him again and again, hoping those prayers would be answered and the ultrasound would finally show he had kidneys and a bladder.

I refused to believe the doctors' report. Throughout the entire pregnancy I didn't believe my baby wasn't developing all his organs. I knew the doctors had great training and experience, but they still could be wrong, and even if their diagnosis was accurate, it did not limit God.

Other than a small and trusted group of friends, I refused to tell people what was going on. I didn't want to breathe life into the negative report. I didn't want it to be true. It wasn't until I was between six and seven months along that I typed out scriptures I had been praying and gave them to people close to us, asking them to believe with us for a miracle. They all knew something was up, but nobody *really* knew what was happening.

I shielded everyone from the truth: our friends, my two other children, our extended family. Troy was trying to be supportive, but I was in my own world. There came a point when it was like I was living in a bubble. I was praying and holding on to hope. I just knew there was no way God was going to allow this baby to die.

There were times when I would look at Josh and Abigail and think that if I kept loving and mothering them the best I knew

> I came to realize it's possible to be devastated and still have hope.

how, that would change something. I kept thinking maybe that would cause this baby, their brother, to be born with the organs he needed.

I was desperate. I was like a lot of mothers who refuse to believe it when someone says something could be wrong with their baby, or worse, that their child likely won't see life outside the womb. It was like an instinct. I love my children—even through the worst times and unthinkable situations—and that is what I did every single day for this baby. I had to believe God would prove this doctor wrong, not just for my sake but for His—for all our sakes.

I came to realize it's possible to be devastated and still have hope. That hope came solely from my relationship with God. I clung to Him because I needed my faith to carry me through this.

I remember writing about this in my journal.

January 5, 2004

Troy, Josh, Abigail, and I were all in the room as Dr. Miller did the ultrasound. We were all guessing at the sex, if it was a girl or boy. We were so excited. Dr. Miller asked the nurse to take the children to the other room. As I was waiting for the children to leave the room, I began to pray quietly in my prayer language, focusing on the Spirit of God. I felt peace, not fear. Although my legs were shaking, my heart and spirit were fixed on Jehovah, my God in whom I trust!

Dr. Miller told us he did not see the baby's kidneys or bladder, or amniotic fluid around the baby. We were shocked but told him we were going to believe God for a miracle—his report would change, and he would see a miracle. I made a promise to pray and journal and speak God's Word in my heart and mind as well as out of my mouth. I knew I could not give up on this baby. I had to have faith for this child within.

One day I would be full of hope. The next, I was in denial. It was a constant mental battle. Each time I would feel the baby move, I held on to my desire for him to be OK. The baby was clearly growing inside me. I was huge throughout this pregnancy. I weighed 180 pounds, and I'm only five foot three. We would laugh hysterically at how big I was. My legs were huge and swollen. Those moments of laughter made me feel normal, as though everything was going to be OK. Yet the reality was that though the baby was getting bigger, I didn't know if he would ever take a breath outside my womb. I didn't know what might happen from day to day.

I simply could not reconcile the two realities—that despite my growing belly and swollen ankles, the child inside me might not live to grow up with his siblings and know me and Troy as his parents. We might not get to lead him in life and faith. I couldn't accept that our time with him might be limited, that I might only have those nine months of mixed emotions, swollen limbs, and prayerful nights of mothering him.

I chose to live in faith, one day at a time, one moment at a time.

I didn't want to believe my life with him would not extend beyond this pregnancy. It was too much for me to wrap my head and heart around. I had to hold on to faith—for me, for this baby, for our family.

My faith kept me sane. I honestly cannot imagine

going through something like that without Jesus, the anchor to my soul—my life raft! I knew what the doctors were telling me; I heard all the medical terms. There were days when it seemed all I could think about was the heavy reality we were facing, but I was trying so hard not to live in those moments.

Instead, I turned to a greater strength to believe bigger. I chose to live in faith, one day at a time, one moment at a time. I had no other choice because the magnitude of what was happening was too great.

That didn't make what happened next any easier. Two words would change our lives, and something once foreign to us would suddenly become our entire world: Potter syndrome.

Chapter 5

The VALLEY

I will ask the Father, and He will give you another Helper (Comforter, Advocate, Intercessor—Counselor, Strengthener, Standby), to be with you forever.

—JOHN **14:16**, AMP

tracyduhon.com/videos/ch5

IT WAS JANUARY 20, 2004. I was twenty-three weeks along. Dr. Kennedy had diagnosed the baby with Potter syndrome, but this was the first time I was to meet Dr. Bennie. I had also seen a maternal fetal specialist, Dr. Joseph Miller, from Louisiana State University. In those early weeks following the first ultrasound, I was getting opinions and gathering as much information as I could, hoping someone would determine the initial diagnosis was not true.

Within five minutes of meeting Dr. Bennie, I knew God had brought him into my life. At the time, I had no idea all the twists and turns we would navigate together, but he was with us every step of the way. He was an answer to my prayers.

I felt peace when I spoke with Dr. Bennie. He was professional and honest about what he saw from my reports, but he felt like a family member who was choosing to walk with me and Troy through the toughest challenge we had faced in our lives. During that visit he gave me the first of many scriptures he would share with me on this journey: "Trust in the LORD with all your heart and do not lean on your own understanding. In all your ways acknowledge Him, and He will make your paths straight" (Prov. 3:5–6).

I left the doctor's office with my faith strengthened, knowing the Lord would be with me through every step of this journey!

I asked Dr. Bennie to share his memories of that first doctor visit.

> I remember the first time Tracy came into my office. I knew she had seen Dr. Miller and Dr. Kennedy and that we were facing a near-impossible situation.
>
> I tell people that my job as an ob-gyn is 90 percent boredom and 10 percent sheer terror. Tracy fell into the latter category. She was diagnosed with having an infant with Potter syndrome, which medically means the baby has no kidneys or bladder. It is a very rare condition that I had seen only one other time in my forty-five years of practice. Many doctors have never seen it and will never see it throughout the duration of their careers. It's a rarity, a strike of lightning.
>
> When a diagnosis of Potter syndrome is made, the circumstances are sensitive because the infant usually survives for only a few hours—one day at most. As a doctor, you are navigating a patient through the horrific reality that they will have only a limited amount of time with the child they are carrying. With Potter syndrome the child's kidneys don't develop, so the amniotic fluid is extremely low, creating changes in the baby, but the main result is that the lungs don't grow or develop properly.
>
> Contributing to its rarity is the fact that Potter syndrome is usually only found in male infants. Nobody really knows why; that just happens to be

the case. The fact that Tracy had already delivered one healthy baby boy made this diagnosis even more rare and perplexing.

When Tracy walked through the doors of our practice, she had a presence about her. She was tenacious. She had already had two previous pregnancies that were normal. This pregnancy was complicated enough, but adding to its complexity was placenta previa. It certainly wasn't as serious as Potter syndrome, but it could lead to severe hemorrhaging and compounded an already difficult pregnancy. Due to the risks, along with Tracy's maternal age, I offered the option to have a hysterectomy. Tracy was having no part of it. She wouldn't even entertain the discussion.

Tracy had a faith that was unshakable. It carried her. It carried all of us. Even amid accepting the reality that the child she was carrying would not survive, she held on to hope and her faith that she would have another pregnancy. She simply believed, so that was how it was. Her faith was evident in everything Tracy did. She and Troy were both walking by faith, not sight. They had this acceptance of the bigger picture; this baby was God's child. Through an extremely difficult situation, they both held on to faith in a circumstance that many would have let destroy them. It was beautiful to witness. At a time when many people would crumble and likely question God or even turn away from Him, they turned to Him even more. It was hard, but they knew God was in charge.

As a doctor, I have two priorities. First, I want to walk patients through the medical side of their journey and help them understand what is happening. But more importantly, we take care of the whole person. It isn't just about the pregnancy or the baby. Tracy knew what was happening to her and her baby, yet she had a grace about her. I wanted to support her in this walk.

When I think about Tracy, the words that come to mind are *grace* and *bold faith*. She was so strong through all of it. She exhibited a remarkable strength. I know there were likely weak moments at home behind closed doors, but not once did she break emotionally when she was with me. I walked alongside her, trusting God through all those months leading up to the delivery.

Despite knowing the enormity of what we were facing, she believed bigger. She inspired all of us— through the most horrific, the most unthinkable circumstances.

Dr. Bennie was an absolute godsend to me and our family. Both accomplished in the medical community and a man of sincere faith, he was a light through the darkness. He brought life to me every time I talked with him, though the report did not change and at times seemed even darker. Dr. Bennie cared for me as a whole person. Not once did I feel as if I was just another patient; I felt as though I was his only patient, even a family member. He reflects the heart of God for people, and it made all the difference in my life. I couldn't have endured any of what we faced without the steadfast support and encouragement of Dr. Bennie and his team.

He was never unrealistic about the situation, but because he believed in something greater, I was able to hold on to my own faith through it. He communicated with care and concern, not gloom and doom. Each time I walked through his office doors, I knew without a doubt that my baby and I would be cared for both medically and spiritually. It was truly a gift to have a doctor who knows his life and the lives of his patients are held in the hands of a loving Father who never leaves or forsakes us and through whom all things are possible.

The Lord would be with me through every step of this journey!

I could have walked away from the experience devastated. There were certainly times when I asked God why. I didn't understand, but what I began to see is that I could feel the pain and fear and uncertainty and simultaneously hold on to faith. I could be broken but still feel loved. I could be angry yet have peace. I could be hurt and still be kind. God was using this deep pain to change me from the inside out. There was a reason for all we were going through.

I understood the prognosis, but I still hoped that when this baby arrived, he would be OK. I held on to that hope until the moment he entered this world.

Chapter 6

The FIRST GOODBYE

I will go to him, but he will not return to me.

—2 Samuel 12:23, MEV

tracyduhon.com/videos/ch6

WHEN HOPE IS ALL YOU HAVE

JONATHON WAS BORN via C-section on May 6, 2004.
In the months leading up to the delivery, the nights were long. I couldn't sleep. I was constantly praying and seeking God and His Word. My home had to be a safe place for me so I wouldn't lose it. I mean, a part of me had already lost it, but spending time with the Lord in prayer and worship gave me peace. When I would allow my thoughts to wander, they were overwhelming.

I understood the science of the situation, but medical explanations didn't help me. I needed God to carry me, and that is exactly how I made it through. There were so many moments when I just wanted to check out. I knew I couldn't, but a part of me wanted to.

As hard as the situation was for me, I know Troy was in just as much pain. I asked him to share some of what he was going through leading up to our son's birth, and from this point on, he will periodically share his perspective on what we were experiencing.

TROY

I was so excited to learn Tracy was pregnant again, and I vividly remember the day we went in for the initial ultrasound. When the nurse and doctor came back into the room, it was almost as if they were at their own funeral. The atmosphere in the room and their demeanor completely changed.

It was as though all life was sucked out of the room. I remember going from a place of pure excitement to depression and deep sadness.

Tracy's faith was so strong. It was our faith that made us hope. We wanted a solution, a second opinion. After the second ultrasound the bottom line for me was that I still had hope, but it was fading.

When Tracy said she wanted to change doctors, I knew she needed to be around someone who could support and encourage her, who would be with her through this without the gloom and doom. I am not a doctor, so I couldn't do anything about the diagnosis, but I wanted to improve the surroundings for my wife, and we did just that.

Most men have a deep desire to protect and please their wives, and when it seems someone or something outside their control is going to hurt them, they'll move into a very protective space. But when the threat is a medical diagnosis, you simply feel helpless.

I wasn't without hope, but I felt helpless. All I wanted to do was protect Tracy, but I knew we needed a miracle.

Tracy began to believe our son would be OK and didn't want to hear anything negative. She believed the diagnosis was wrong or that God was going to miraculously save the baby. She was professing Scripture and trusting God's Word. She believed beyond a shadow of a doubt that somehow the baby would be healthy.

I always felt her faith was stronger than mine, but I was truly standing with her. I didn't deny her hope. I encouraged her, but deep down I knew we would need God to intervene miraculously because every medical explanation was against us.

I remember going in to deliver Jonathon. We left early in the morning while both kids were still sleeping. The drive to the hospital was quiet and sobering. I was concerned, but we continued to pray. Troy and I did our part. We kept believing. We kept praying. We supported each other.

I had heard for the past seven months, "He is going to die." I still didn't know if I believed what the doctors were saying, but either way I wasn't going to give up on him. I wanted our baby to live; I wanted to hold him. I still wanted a miracle, so I kept praying.

Our friends loved and prayed for us. My family did the same. They all helped us carry the weight of what we were facing. Nobody could give me answers, but their love and support meant everything. As I remember those moments, I think about women who go through hard times without love and support, and I want to just wrap my arms around them because I know how crucial the care of friends and family was to my survival. I *needed* it. I was standing in faith, believing for a miracle, but I still needed our friends and family to love me through the darkness.

When we arrived at the hospital, so many of our friends and family were already in the waiting room. Troy was with me as I was being prepped for surgery. My mother was also with us. She was in the room for both Joshua's and Abigail's births. My dad was in the waiting area with everyone else. My entire family and our dear friends were all there to love us through this.

Sometimes God says yes. Sometimes He says no. Sometimes we are asked to wait.

It was just days before Mother's Day.

Dr. Bennie exhibited such a peace throughout the procedure. When I think back on that day, I can't thank God enough that he was the one in that delivery room with me and Troy. Throughout the entire pregnancy he communicated the medical realities to us without quashing our hope or minimizing our faith. That is exactly the kind of doctor I needed that day.

I was given an epidural, and the C-section was like the others. I had done that before. That was the easy part. The hard part came after the baby arrived. My mother left the room, fearing the worst and knowing it was too much for her to watch if the baby didn't make it.

Jonathon was a beautiful boy. When he was born, he

didn't cry. They rushed him straight out of the room. As I watched the doctors and nurses move swiftly, taking him away from me, I looked up and said, "Lord, I trust You."

Forty-five minutes later they brought him back to me. He was on machines and breathing slowly. They confirmed everything I was trying to pray away. I just couldn't believe it. "God, please let him live," I prayed. I didn't want to let him go.

Sometimes God says yes. Sometimes He says no. Sometimes we are asked to wait.

This was a no.

Jonathon lived only an hour.

As I was holding him, I just felt helpless. The grief was too much. I was devastated. When they laid him on my chest, he was no longer hooked up to the machines. The room was quiet and somber. Nobody knew what to say. We all knew these would be his final moments.

I was so happy to hold him, love him, be his mama. I was holding him when he took his last breath. I was resting and calm, the peace of the Lord covering me and doing for me what I couldn't do for myself. Even as he lay still in my arms, I didn't let him go. I just held him.

TROY

We already had two children, so we knew what a normal delivery should look and feel like. When we walked in the hospital, there was standing room only in the waiting area. This was clearly not normal. There were two doctors and several nurses—it was all hands on deck.

As soon as Jonathon arrived, they rushed him to another room. I caught a glimpse of him as they took him away. His eyes were closed. He looked like me. I thought he looked so normal; maybe this was all a mistake. Would we get our miracle?

When they brought him back to Tracy, they confirmed the worst and explained what was going to happen. For me, that was one of the most difficult moments—when they told us Jonathon was going to die. I just stood there wanting to protect Tracy. She wanted to hold him. I remember thinking if I couldn't do anything to make him live, I'd protect Tracy's emotions. I'd help her spend as much time with him as she could.

It was a very emotionally difficult time. I felt the weight of knowing this precious baby Tracy was holding was going to die. I wanted so badly to take that pain away.

He didn't live long, and even after he passed, Tracy didn't want to let him go. She wouldn't let him go. It was tough. She looked at me when she finally handed him back to the doctor, tears in her eyes. I just held her. It was one of those moments you just can't believe. It felt surreal, like a bad dream. I hoped I would wake up to find none of this was actually happening.

As a man, I felt I was supposed to be strong. I wanted to tell my wife it was going to be OK. I wanted to make sense of it for her, to be her light and her encourager, but it was so hard. I could hardly talk past the lump in my throat. We knew God had a plan, but how could this be it? The pain was so excruciating I felt a numbness wash over me.

I don't remember giving Jonathon back to the doctor. I was holding him, and then I sat up. In that moment, I felt as if Jesus said it was OK to let him go. I sensed the heavens opening up to receive him. It was as if a ray of light had entered a room filled with great sorrow. I was tired, and everyone thought I was hallucinating, but I know what I saw. It was a moment of beauty in the darkness.

The room was full of people, and we were each experiencing an array of emotions. I had just given birth, but the physical pain paled in comparison to the emotional pain I was feeling—that everyone was feeling. It was overwhelming, crushing even.

We don't have video of Jonathon's birth. Nobody could even fathom taking videos or photos with so much happening.

I dressed him, crying all the while, barely able to see through the tears. We took a photo of Jonathon wearing that little outfit. It is the only picture we have of our precious boy.

That night was so quiet and sad, but the next day was worse. I had been given medication to help me sleep through the night, and when I woke up, I had to relive the nightmare. The beautiful child I had carried, mothered, and loved for months wouldn't be going home with me. I was in the hospital with all the signs of childbirth—the weight gain, the pain from the C-section—but no baby. I was trying to accept the truth but wasn't fully able to process all that had happened.

Everyone was so kind and caring. Dr. Bennie came to talk to me, and I felt his sincerity. He reflected the love of God during that time, and he helped me do the same. I was devastated and broken, but when people came to see me, I wanted to love them. I didn't want to be angry with God, and I wasn't angry at Him—at least not yet.

I was in the hospital for five days, surrounded by everything that reminded me of what we had lost. I wanted to be anywhere else. I couldn't pray. I was a woman of faith, but I just couldn't do anything in those days. Although I felt completely numb and unable to do anything but simply breathe, I knew God loved me. I could feel it.

My friend Tony put a keepsake in my hand that featured a scripture from the Book of Romans.

> Now may God, the fountain of hope, fill you to overflowing with uncontainable joy and perfect peace as you trust in him. And may the power of the Holy Spirit continually surround your life with his super-abundance until you radiate with hope!
>
> —ROMANS 15:13, TPT

That verse meant so much to me. Everything given or spoken to me during that time was in some way giving me life, which I desperately needed.

I did not realize it then, but in the month to come the Lord would remind me of that scripture. He prompted me to write it down, and I seized on the word *hope*. It gave my life new meaning and is the foundation on which Giving Hope was eventually built.

Have you ever found yourself in a place that was so dark it felt beyond God's reach? Have you cried out in the darkness, wanting your reality to be something different? That is how I felt, but despite the weight of what we had gone through, I knew God was with me. I made it my aim to listen for His voice, direct my focus to see Him, and allow myself to just be still, just as the

Lord said in His Word: "Be still and know that I am God" (Ps. 46:10, MEV).

If you're in the midst of pain that seems unbearable, be still and wait on God. You will find Him.

GOING HOME

On the drive home I felt as if I were in a fog. I cried and cried, wondering if the last five days had really happened. The pain was so intense. We were headed home from the hospital, and there was no baby with us. I kept staring at my empty arms, my tears running from my cheek and falling onto my open palms.

The drive felt like an eternity. At every stoplight and turn, I kept wanting to look back at our baby boy in his car seat to make sure he was OK. But he wasn't there. At home I didn't want to eat. I didn't want anything except to have my Jonathon with us.

> If you're in the midst of pain that seems unbearable, be still and wait on God. You will find Him.

The kids knew there was no baby, that their brother didn't come home with Mommy and Daddy from the hospital, and my heart hurt for both of them. I was still trying to process everything myself as well, and the kids noticed. Josh said he wasn't going to stop kissing me until I stopped crying.

Troy and I didn't know how to walk through the loss of our son or how to process our grief, and we certainly had no capacity to explain to our precious children what had happened. In those early days after coming home from the hospital, I just wanted to wrap Josh and Abigail up in my arms and never let go! They gave me hope. I love them more than anything, and in a way they helped me survive because they gave me meaning and purpose beyond the pain.

The emptiness in my heart and soul was like nothing I had ever experienced. At one point I screamed, hoping it would make me feel better. It didn't. Nothing made it better. I felt hurt and broken, and I was angry.

Even though I was weak, I reached out to God. In one of my first journal entries after Jonathon died, I asked God to fill me with something I wondered if I'd ever feel again—joy.

May 15, 2004

Sorrow into joy, Lord. I ask You humbly to take away the sadness and fill me with Your joy—the joy only You can give—for one of the things other than You that I value passionately is gone from here. Please help me to move forward with joy. Help me to trust You more. Take the ache in my arms and use it for Your eternal purpose.

Chapter 7

IN HIS HANDS

Do not fear, for I am with you; do not anxiously look about you, for I am your God. I will strengthen you, surely I will help you, surely I will uphold you with My righteous right hand.

—Isaiah 41:10

tracyduhon.com/videos/ch7

NOBODY KNEW WHAT to say. With each passing day the reality of our loss set in more and more. I didn't know how to live; sometimes it was a struggle just to breathe or even to care for my other children. I looked after them because that is what a mother does, but I wanted our beautiful Jonathon to be with us. I wanted to nurse him, change him, watch him interact with his brother and sister. There was such a void in my heart and our home.

I went back to the hospital a week later, as I was still healing from the C-section. I cannot say enough about the hospital staff and Dr. Bennie—they carried me through all of it. When all I felt was emptiness and despair, they loved me, and I wanted to love them back. I was never angry with any of them. I knew they had done all they could to help me, and they were still helping me.

As the days passed, I realized I was angry with someone—God. I loved Him, but I was so angry. I wanted to scream, "Why did You let this happen to me, to us?" While I couldn't deny the peace I felt when I turned to Him, I was still angry.

But I didn't know if it was acceptable to be angry at God, so I channeled all that emotion into reaching out to others. To show my gratitude, I made keepsake plaques for the nurses and doctors in memory of Jonathon. They said:

"For I know the plans I have for you," declares
the LORD, "plans to prosper you and not to harm
you, plans to give you hope and a future."
—JEREMIAH 29:11, NIV

From hearts filled with love and appreciation, we
would like to say thank you, as we know God
chose you to assist us with the birth of our son,
and we give Him all the glory.
TROY & TRACY DUHON

Each person on the hospital staff received one. My
heart was heavy, but those words were true: we couldn't
thank them enough for the way they cared for us and
Jonathon.

A CELEBRATION OF LIFE

I never wanted a funeral. The situation was sad enough.
I didn't want to see the blank stares when people didn't
know what to say. I felt as though everyone would be
looking at me but I still wouldn't truly be seen. What
do you say to a woman who just lost a baby she carried to term? There are simply no words. That made it
worse.

Yet I saw this as an opportunity to love my son and
love him well, to send him off and celebrate his life.
So though I was still healing from the C-section and
feeling the emptiness of losing our son, we decided to
hold a service at our church.

There were hundreds of people there, some whom we hadn't seen in years. They were just as angry and confused as we were. I also knew that because we were a family of faith, they were looking to see how we would respond. What would we do? I knew they tried to relate to what we were walking through, wondering how they would handle it, but it is impossible unless you have experienced it yourself. It is easy to think you're saying all the right things when you're not the one navigating the pain and loss.

It is easy to think you're saying all the right things when you're not the one navigating the pain and loss.

Our pastor spoke and then invited me to say a few words. I had asked to do so because it would be my last opportunity to mother my son and share him with the world, or so I thought.

God was working through me as I spoke that day. The words just came. They kept coming. I went on and on. Everything in me wanted to hide away with my pain, but as I stood there, a strength washed over me. I felt the presence of the Lord. I didn't want all eyes on me, but I was determined to speak on Jonathon's behalf, to let people know how fragile life can be and that we need to be thankful for every day we have with loved ones. It was a message I would continue to carry long after that service.

I sat as I spoke because I was still in a lot of pain, but I needed to share the gospel. It was the only thing I knew to do. My words were vulnerable, transparent, and genuine.

Despite feeling as if our family was on display, I must admit, the service was beautiful—the music, the message, all of it. The Spirit of God moved in that room.

Losing Jonathon left me feeling weak. I had strength the day of the funeral, but it was fleeting. I had to accept that this was my new reality.

One good thing is that the experience drew Troy and me closer. At a time when many couples would turn from each other, we were able to turn to each other. Something beautiful was growing between us, a deeper level of closeness and friendship we always hoped to have. We realized that in his short time on earth, Jonathon made a life-changing impact on his dad and mom. We would never be the same, and some of those changes were for the better. In time we would work together to build from our painful journey something that would touch a hurting world.

It is hard to admit all these years later, but there were times when I felt dead. God's love and the love of family and friends filled my heart and helped me keep going even when I did not know how I could do that. Until Jonathon I didn't truly know the power of love to heal a broken heart. I wanted to be left alone, but God wouldn't allow it. His love and the love of those around me kept pouring in. Each time I wanted to turn my face and hide, the Lord and our friends and family were there.

During those early months I kept going to the Scriptures, studying and dissecting them in an attempt to make sense of what had happened to Jonathon. "*Lord, what is eternal life?*" I wondered. I was desperate for answers, and I knew they needed to come from God. I saw the psalmist's words, "I shall not die, but live, and declare the works of the Lord" (Ps. 118:17, kjv), and I knew that to die is to live. My son was no longer on this earth, but he was alive and well in heaven.

I couldn't do much, but I could talk to God.

As I was processing all this, I kept asking and seeking. I would scream, "What do You want me to do, Lord?" Every emotion I was feeling was wrapped in those sentiments.

The answer was Joshua and Abigail.

God needed me to be faithful with what was already in my hands, but it was hard. Sometimes I didn't know if I had it in me. I was on my knees, praying, "God, help me! Help me to be their mother." I was devastated and lost, but I couldn't stay in that place. Joshua and Abigail needed me too.

I was still healing from the physical effects of pregnancy and the C-section, so Joshua, Abigail, and I spent much of my recuperation time watching movies. I ordered as many videos as I could find on all kinds of subjects: history, science, the Bible—anything we could snuggle up with and learn from. That was how I homeschooled them while I was still recovering. It was the only way I knew to spend time with them when the physical and emotional pain were weighing me down.

For a while the Scriptures were just words on a page. I couldn't read the Bible. I could barely pray. I felt empty and hollow.

That's when I began to understand how loving and powerful God truly is. I couldn't do much, but I could talk to God. I could turn to my Abba Father, and I found that He was there for me and with me.

I felt God's presence all around me. What I'd read about in the Bible became real to me. He was my "refuge and strength, a very present help in trouble" (Ps. 46:1, ESV). He was—and is—there in every moment. I felt the love of God. He didn't need me to do anything to pour His love on me. In the midst of my anger and grief, He loved me back to life.

OPENING MY HEART

I protected myself and my heart for the next two years as I was going through the painful process of learning to live again after loss.

I wanted to isolate myself and disappear, but God wouldn't allow it. We were well loved by our spiritual family, and our home was filled with that love—and so much stuff. People kept checking on us, bringing meals and gifts. I began to see that while we live in a broken world, God uses all of us and our stories, as painful and difficult as some of them may be, to bring healing. We are to carry His message and make Him known to those around us.

My pain allowed me to begin to see others who were hurting. I noticed people looking at me with longing in their eyes, not knowing what to say. Instead of approaching me, they would turn away. Anyone who has been through a loss of any kind knows this all too well. At one point I made buttons with that lone photo of Jonathon that said, "Ask me." It was my way of inviting people to ask me about the baby I lost.

God uses all of us and our stories, as painful and difficult as some of them may be, to bring healing.

That button allowed me to step into a place of openness and vulnerability. Losing a child can unite any two mothers, no matter how different or similar their lives may be, though it's a bond you'd prefer not to share. After surviving losing Jonathon, I could see people's pain more clearly. I found a willingness to talk with others and learn from those who were walking through their own pain.

Now I can almost immediately tell when people are hurting, and I am able to empathize. This is one of the most profound ways God changed me. Even if I can't relate to the specific trial someone is going through, I can draw from my experience to meet them on some level.

Over time I began to understand that God brings purpose out of our pain. Even if we haven't experienced the same thing as someone else, we recognize the hurt. Showing this type of compassion can change lives. When we are struggling, the kindness of even one person can make a world of difference. It can open a door to hope and remind someone that they're not the only one.

We are never alone in our pain.

TROY

When we got home, the church rallied around us and was wonderful. Our pastors coached us, trying to help us understand.

When something devastating happens, you always

have questions. What sin am I paying for? What did I do wrong, God? Is this because of what I did ten years ago? The enemy tends to rewind the film of your life and get you playing the blame game, but his specialty is lies. For weeks and months all I could think was, "What did I do?" I blamed myself.

Tracy wanted answers. She wanted to know why we lost Jonathon—why he had Potter syndrome in the first place. I wanted to be the one to make sense of it for her, though all the while I was questioning God myself and trying to rationalize the enormity of what had happened.

Tracy's faith was extremely strong. She began to believe that God was planning something bigger, that He would not allow her to go through this without having something on the other side of the mountain.

Three to four months after Jonathon left us, Tracy started to believe there was a purpose for the pain. The pain for her was massive, but she truly connected with other women and started making grief baskets for people. She didn't want anyone to face what we went through alone, so she made the "Ask me" buttons.

We slowly began to get back to life.

THROUGH THE GRIEF

The summer after Jonathon passed, our friends surrounded us. We made memories. I remember swimming with the kids. Little by little I was coming back to life.

The sense of loss was still there, and my heart was still hurting, but I was being loved. It was life-giving. It was a rough time, but it was filled with so much love. I knew I would forever feel the hole of not having Jonathon with us, but I learned to live through the grief and focus on what was right in front of me: my husband and our two children. Life went on.

We never thought our life together would take such a tragic turn, but we walked through it together.

But grief isn't linear. You don't just go through it, and you're done. Grief often comes in waves.

Christmas 2004 was hard. A part of me was present, and another part of me was lost in grief. It had only been seven months since Jonathon had gone to heaven.

We were having our Christmas cards made, and I wanted to include him. He was still a part of our family, a part of me. I worked with an artist to include him in the card using the photo we had taken at the hospital. He looked like a ghost, but I didn't care. I sent out the cards anyway. I was his mother, and he was my baby.

Even with the loss, the desire of my heart was still to have more babies. I loved Joshua and Abigail, but my vision for our family hadn't changed.

Troy and I had grown so much closer. We never thought our life together would take such a tragic turn, but we walked through it together. We were devastated but still walking. And we saw God was in all of it, bringing us to the other side of loss.

We saw God was in all of it, bringing us to the other side of loss.

The friendship and strength we gained as a couple in the months after Jonathon passed prepared us for more devastation that would wreak havoc on our lives: Hurricane Katrina.

Chapter 8

The LORD GIVETH

And hope does not disappoint, because the love of God has been poured out within our hearts through the Holy Spirit who was given to us.

—ROMANS 5:5

tracyduhon.com/videos/ch8

AFTER JONATHON'S PASSING, my idea of what my life was supposed to look like changed. I knew there would no longer be babies every three years. I still wanted four children, but I knew I had no control over how that would happen, so I did my best to surrender and simply follow the Lord's lead.

Jonathon left us in May 2004, and by August 2005, we were preparing to sell our house on Paris Avenue. Life was going on, and we had decided to build a new home. We also started the process to potentially adopt and were on a waiting list. My heart for a big family hadn't changed; my circumstances had. I was looking for something to hope for.

The thought of leaving Paris Avenue evoked so many emotions, both good and bad. Troy and I had started our life together there. We brought our first two children to that house. We had beautiful memories there, even though some were now compounded by loss. We would soon gain an even deeper understanding of loss, but at the time, we thought we had gone through the worst.

Troy and I both grew up in New Orleans, so we had been through hurricanes. But when we were told there was a mandatory evacuation, we knew this one wasn't typical. I don't know that any of us who had grown up in New Orleans could have imagined what would follow. We knew Katrina was bad, but we didn't know it would be *that* bad.

Troy and I were going back and forth between Paris Avenue and the new house when we learned of the evacuation order. We decided to stay with Troy's parents, who had a home about three hours away in Lafayette, Louisiana.

We were supposed to fully move into the new house the weekend Hurricane Katrina hit. The new house represented a fresh start, and I was so ready to get into it. But this hurricane could not be ignored. Our plan was that I would head to Lafayette with the kids, and Troy would come later, after wrapping up some things at work. As I was packing up the kids and the car, I grabbed one box of keepsakes—*one box*. To this day I am thankful I did. I didn't know it then, but it would be the only thing left of our life after Katrina. It was a box filled with CDs, videos, DVDs, and photos of our children—all of them.

Josh and Abigail were in the car with me. I still laugh when I think back to our evacuation, because we looked like the family from *The Beverly Hillbillies*. The car was as packed as it could be. I had everything I would need for the kids: blankets, clothes, snacks.

Traffic was backed up with so many people trying to make it out of New Orleans. I was on the Baton Rouge bridge for what seemed like hours. Traffic was not moving. Imagine hundreds of thousands of people all making their way out of the city. There were only a few routes out of New Orleans, and the bridge was one of them.

When we left, I didn't realize traffic would be that bad. I had one of those thirty-two-ounce Big Gulp cups of Diet Coke and had been drinking it, not realizing a bathroom stop would be out of the question. When you are told to leave your home and that you have a short window of time to do so, you naturally go into survival mode. I had the babies. I had everything they needed. I had everything I needed. I had my box. I just had no idea how long the trip would take or how long we would be staying in Lafayette. We honestly thought we would be staying with Troy's parents long enough to ride out the storm and then life would get back to normal.

Nothing about Katrina was normal.

Once I realized we were stuck on that bridge and would be for quite a while, I regretted the massive cup of Diet Coke. I am a mom, and as you might imagine, I did whatever the moment called for. In that moment, I needed to go to the bathroom, but pulling over was not an option. So I went in that cup—*twice.*

I had to go so badly I dumped out my drink and went right there in the car. I didn't care. The kids had no idea, and I was trying to be discreet so no one around me could see either. I was so preoccupied with trying to make it off that bridge and get the kids to safety that it didn't even dawn on me until after we arrived at Troy's parents' house later that day that I may have had to go to the bathroom so bad because I was pregnant.

It had only been a year since Jonathon's birth. I was still processing that loss and trying to navigate through life, the new house, the kids, Troy's work. I was still grieving and protecting myself and our family. While another baby had been on my heart, it was an afterthought during the grief.

Once we all finally arrived at Troy's parents' house, we were watching the news as the storm made landfall. I felt nauseated. A part of me believed it was simply due to spending all those hours in the car and realizing the magnitude of Katrina, but somewhere inside my mommy heart, I had a fleeting thought. *Could I be?*

I took a test. I was apprehensive and didn't allow myself to think it could really be positive. But the result was clear: I was pregnant again!

I honestly believed I would never get pregnant again, so I was genuinely excited. I had no fear or hesitation. I had been trying to figure out why God allowed us to go through the loss of Jonathon, and this silenced those questions. God was giving us beauty for ashes, the oil of joy for mourning. He was redeeming our loss and breathing life back into all of us. There was no caution. I was overjoyed. It was that simple.

I had *no idea* what was to come.

For all those months carrying Jonathon, I lived by

faith. Even when the doctor's report was negative, I dared to believe. When I had to accept the reality that we didn't get the miracle we were seeking, my faith was challenged. I was angry and confused. But I still had a feeling of peace and comfort because I had faith. Having faith does not mean you are immune to anger and confusion. It means you can experience peace that you don't understand in the midst of it. With God, in the midst of my greatest grief I had the greatest peace.

I was pregnant again, and I knew this baby was God showing up to bring me back to life.

I told Troy and his parents the news.

TROY

It was August 2005. I had been through hurricanes before, but never in my memory had there been a mandatory requirement to evacuate. We had to leave. Tracy was going to pack up and leave early with the two kids. I was trying to prepare the dealerships the best I could and planned to leave later.

I left New Orleans at around 2:00 p.m., and it took nine hours to get to Lafayette, a drive that typically takes three hours, give or take. When I arrived, I was thankful we had all made it and that Tracy and the kids were safe.

When we turned on the news, it looked as if everything was underwater. At first, we didn't even know what we were looking at. The magnitude of Katrina was just beginning to hit us. It seemed like the entire city was underwater. As a business owner, I began to fear that my business would not survive the devastation. That kind of fear can be paralyzing.

The first time I saw the dealerships was on TV. A news crew was in a helicopter reporting from an aerial view because there was too much flooding to drive through the city. I looked at the dealerships and thought, "Oh my goodness! All the cars are gone!" And then I looked again. The cars were all there, but they were underwater. I was overcome by so many emotions—fear, loss, dread—I began to cry. My business was my baby, and it looked like everything I had worked for was gone.

A year before, we lost our son. Now this. It was too much to comprehend, and it hit me all at once.

I still remember my dad looking at me in that fatherly way of his as I was on the ground crying. He pointed at the TV and said, "Son, the brick and mortar comes and goes; the franchises will come and go too. You go back and take care of your employees; take care of your people. That is what matters. That is what God calls you to do."

There was something in his words that changed me that night. His words were placed on my heart, and I began to see the bigger picture and the opportunity to care for people.

WHEN HOPE IS ALL YOU HAVE

I was going back and forth from Lafayette to New Orleans, trying to rebuild—three hours there and three hours back every day. We lost everything except one dealership.

When Tracy told me she was pregnant, it was like a light amid all the loss. We felt that this was God's promise. There was so much devastation surrounding us, and we had endured so much over the past year. This was the blessing in all of it, the thing to turn our eyes toward. We were thrilled.

THE STRIKE OF LIGHTNING

Katrina was like nothing any of us had ever experienced or seen. Everything was gone. Both houses were destroyed. We managed to salvage some items, but for the most part both homes were gone. The dealerships were literally underwater. We never could have imagined what Katrina would do to our city, to all the people, and to us. It was awful.

We ended up staying in Lafayette for three months as Troy attempted to rebuild the business and we worked to pick up the pieces of our life following the hurricane. It was a difficult time, trying to make sense of everything while being displaced.

Seeing all that loss brought all the emotions from the past year back, and they hit me like a ton of bricks. It was like the loss of Jonathon and everything I felt was on display in the rubble and destruction that surrounded us. There was loss everywhere. I couldn't escape it.

My pregnancy was our blessing. It gave us hope again.

Troy's hope and faith had carried me through the loss of Jonathon. My hope and faith helped carry him through the devastation of Katrina. God continued to bring us closer in partnership, friendship, and faith.

Those months were difficult for Troy, but he loved his people

What began from a traumatic and painful journey became one of our greatest passions and the purpose for our family: loving people and being the hands and feet of Christ.

well. He took the words of his father and walked in faith, knowing that if he cared for people, the rest would follow. There were so many residents in need during that time too, not only loyal employees but our friends and neighbors.

Eighty percent of New Orleans was flooded. The water destroyed so much, leaving thousands of people who didn't evacuate without food, shelter, and basic necessities.

Our church had approached us about opening a relief center at one of the Honda dealerships. We had already been working with the local food pantry and felt this would be a great opportunity to help. In that first week alone we provided assistance to over a thousand cars a day. It was amazing to see the joy on the faces of both the employees who were serving and those who had lost everything.

I remember Troy coming to me and saying with tears in his eyes, "If God can get us through this, the rest of our lives will be devoted to giving back to the community." Katrina taught us how to love and care for others, even through our own loss.

There was no way God would allow this to happen to us twice. Surely He wouldn't do that.

What began from a traumatic and painful journey became one of our greatest passions and the purpose for our family: loving people well and being the hands and feet of Christ.

This baby was a bright, shining light in all of it. The more we gave, the more fulfilled we were. We were all coming back to life. It was beautiful.

I didn't have any challenges with the pregnancy. There was already so much going on during those days following the hurricane that we were simply trying to find a new rhythm. Not once did the thought cross my mind that something might happen to this baby. I held on to my belief that this child was a beautiful gift from God following the loss of Jonathon. He was bringing beauty out of the ashes.

The hurricane hit at the end of August. By the end of October, we were preparing for the first ultrasound.

We again went to Dr. Bennie's office. I was strong. Seventeen months earlier, I delivered the eulogy at my son's funeral. I spent those months on my hands and knees, my face in my palms, crying out to God. This was God turning it all around, giving me joy for mourning, as Isaiah 61:3 says. I believed that with everything in me.

When we arrived, it felt just as it had before. The faces were familiar; the place was familiar. This was the team that had walked us through the pregnancy with Jonathon, and now here we all were again. It almost felt surreal. There was a joy that filled the halls, as everyone knew what we had endured. I was walking in faith and living in a moment of pure joy.

The same woman on the team who was with me through my pregnancy with Jonathon and ran all the blood work and ultrasounds would be overseeing my ultrasound and blood work again. She was *the* specialist of all specialists. She knew what she was doing.

When she came into the room accompanied by Dr. Bennie, my heart sank. I could see it on their faces— Potter syndrome again. I was in disbelief.

TROY

It was the October after Katrina. We were still navigating through the devastation from the hurricane. The pregnancy kept all of us looking forward with joy. We were trying to rebuild our lives the best we could despite being displaced and walking through so many unknowns.

The baby was a light, a ray of hope as we climbed out from the rubble left in the aftermath of the hurricane and losing Jonathon.

When we went in for the first ultrasound, Tracy didn't have any concerns. The months leading up to that day were calm. She felt good. We believed this baby was God's gift to us, a blessing after all we had lost.

You could have stuck a fork in me when Dr. Bennie told us again that he couldn't see kidneys. I was in complete shock. After everything we had been through, I had a close relationship with Dr. Bennie and knew him quite well. He was in shock too. We were all in shock.

Then I found myself getting angry. "Really, God? Why? Twice? Why us? Why twice?"

My thoughts took over, trying to make sense of it. I must have been a bad Christian, and this was us paying for that. Certainly, this was the mistakes of the past catching up with me. "What did I do, God?"

When I consulted with Dr. Bennie, he said it was like lightning striking twice. Potter syndrome was so rare already, to go through it a second time back-to-back was unheard of. It is so rare, in fact, statistics on it didn't even exist. Dr. Bennie said he had never seen this happen twice.

It was ridiculous, and it was happening to us, this medical anomaly.

"Why us? God, why would You allow this to happen to us? Haven't we been through enough?" I had no idea how we were going to endure this a second time.

I suppressed everything. I was supposed to be strong and compassionate and empathetic, but it was nearly impossible. Underneath it all, I was mad—really mad. This time we knew exactly what to expect, and that almost made it worse.

I questioned the people I trusted most. I wanted answers that nobody seemed to have. "We don't know why God does what He does" is what I kept hearing over and over, and that just angered me further.

Tracy was incredible and handled the news with the same strength and faith that she did the first time. I love that about her.

Even though I was angry, I still had faith in God and believed His power wasn't limited to what the doctors said, but I had so many questions. I needed to make sense of the situation. I was believing, as Tracy was believing, that this baby would be OK. Our faith was all we had to hang on to. We believed together.

There was no way God would allow this to happen to us twice. Surely He wouldn't do that.

From the minute I heard the words *Potter syndrome*, I knew I had to trust God. I am a woman of faith. I went through this once. I could do it again. Despite what we had walked through, I dared to believe the doctors could be wrong. I dared to believe God would not make us go through that pain again. I begged Him not to let us go through that again.

I had to dig even deeper in my faith. I knew how this could go. So I believed bigger. I prayed harder. I just knew God wouldn't allow us to lose another child.

God is always in control, even when we don't understand.

Have you ever been in a situation you were powerless to change and you had no choice but to believe in something greater than yourself? That is how I felt when we received a second diagnosis of Potter syndrome. I tried to pray it away and believe our son would be OK despite what the science was telling us. I thought my faith would sustain us and that everyone else was wrong.

A dear friend of mine had just gone through something similar after a family member had been diagnosed with cancer. She prayed. She believed God. But that didn't change the outcome.

It was a reminder that God is always in control, even when we don't understand. That awareness doesn't make the hurt any less painful, but there is a peace in knowing we are promised life everlasting.

Pause for a moment and reflect on a time when you had to pray harder or believe bigger. What was the outcome? Did you have any control over any of what happened? What did you learn?

If there is one thing I've learned through all we've gone through, it is that God is always with us, especially in our darkest moments.

"The LORD gave and the LORD has taken away; may the name of the LORD be praised" (Job 1:21, NIV).

Chapter 9

FEAR NOT

There is no fear in love; but perfect love casts out fear, because fear involves punishment, and the one who fears is not perfected in love.

—1 John 4:18

Let's Talk

tracyduhon.com/videos/ch9

THE IDEA OF having to walk through the same heartache we experienced with Jonathon was unbearable. I couldn't even let myself go there emotionally. I had buried one son; I wasn't going to do it again.

I wanted to be angry and hold on to the confusion and frustration, but I knew this baby needed his mother as well. I had to hold on to my faith, but with every test and every appointment, it became so difficult. I was praying, but I also began looking for solutions. I researched every possible way to save this baby.

At one point we heard about a procedure in Russia where doctors attempt to inject amniotic fluid into the mother. It may sound extreme, but the idea of losing another baby was incomprehensible to us. We ultimately decided against the procedure, but I wanted so badly to fix it and make it better that I was willing to consider almost anything.

I saw the specialist every three weeks. With Jonathon I had an unwavering faith that carried me through. This time was different because I knew what could happen. I had been there. I had done it. I never lost hope in God. He was giving me strength day by day. But I just knew. I felt it. A mother knows.

Over the course of those months, there were so many moments that took me back to missing Jonathon. I would think about him while trying to love the baby inside me. I was trying to love him to life. It was all so familiar.

Dr. Bennie walked us through this pregnancy with the same love and care. I never felt the gloom and doom of the situation. The pregnancy itself was very different from Jonathon's. I had a complete previa this time, which meant my entire cervix was obstructed, and doctors were recommending a hysterectomy after the baby was born, but the pregnancy itself felt normal. It was all pretty routine, other than the fact that we were praying daily that the baby would survive long enough for us to meet him or that we might get our miracle.

I believed God could create the organs our baby lacked, but because I knew the medical realities, I also began to wrap my head around saying goodbye for a second time. I don't know that it's really possible to prepare to lose a child, but I tried.

Imagine learning you are pregnant and being overjoyed that you will welcome a beautiful baby into your family, but it doesn't happen. Instead, you give birth but are never able to take the baby home. You are left with only the memory of the nine months you carried him, the delivery experience, and the few moments you were able to hold him before he took his last breath— nothing more.

Now imagine having to do it twice.

TROY

We made it through Jonathon, but I kept wondering how we could possibly endure that much pain again.

The doctors were running all these tests, trying to understand the diagnosis. The first time around was uncommon. The second was unheard of. Medically, everyone was trying to make sense of it. There were simply no answers to be found.

We ran some tests at Children's Hospital. They wanted to study how this could potentially happen twice and were looking at our DNA for genetic patterns. We were working with one of the chief doctors in the hospital. When he brought me the results, I didn't even want to look. He said I had a bad X chromosome, and that was the only explanation they had.

We even questioned that. We'd had a healthy baby boy, our first son, Joshua. If it was all on me, why did we have two healthy children, especially our son? Everyone was trying to make sense of it medically, but it still didn't add up.

At the same time, we were trying to figure out how we could fix it. We were even offered an opportunity to go to Russia to get amniotic fluid injected.

The entire time, I was questioning. "Really? Why, God? Why?"

I followed Tracy's lead because left to my own devices, I would have been swallowed whole by my anger. It was there, but I became really good at shoving it down. I learned that by pushing it away, I didn't have to feel it. So I kept pushing.

I was in shock and denial up until the day he was born. I was numb, and it all felt surreal. But the delivery was a completely different experience from the first time around.

THE LONG GOODBYE

"Affliction will not rise up a second time." I lived by that promise in Nahum 1:9 (NKJV) and read it over and over from the day the diagnosis was made until the day I gave birth. I had to believe, but it was hard.

I prayed for months—for the diagnosis to be wrong, for God to redeem our suffering, for a miracle. I prayed that God would allow this baby to be whole. I prayed we would get to meet him on this side

I just knew. I felt it. A mother knows.

of heaven, just as we had gotten to do with Jonathon.

It was May 4, 2006, exactly two years to the day that we lost Jonathon.

I was scheduled to have another C-section. The drive to the hospital was eerily familiar. We were all very quiet—hopeful, but quiet. Nobody would say how they were feeling. For months I wouldn't allow anyone to speak negatively and say we would lose the baby. I knew the reality, but I wasn't giving up hope.

At the hospital we were again surrounded by so many people who loved us—close friends, our pastors, and family. My mother wasn't in the delivery room this time. Losing Jonathon was just too much for her, and she couldn't imagine having to go through that again.

Dr. Bennie delivered a beautiful baby boy: Joseph Jeremiah.

It was Troy who delivered the news to me: Joseph wasn't expected to make it.

In that delivery room something took over me. I doubted the doctors. I doubted everything. "Are you sure?" I kept asking over and over. I knew the doctors were well trained and capable, but I still doubted.

When they took him off the ultrasound machine they were using to check for his kidneys and lungs, I kept looking at the screen. I wanted them to please keep checking for kidneys. It felt as if I watched that screen for an eternity. Then Dr. Bennie confirmed the worst: Joseph had no kidneys, and his lungs had not developed.

Despite all our research, all our prayers, all our belief, the result was the same. Although I knew this could be the outcome, it was a hard reality to accept.

As they took Joseph away to run tests, I heard him cry. Jonathon had passed so quickly they weren't able to run any tests. This time the medical team wanted to do what they could to make sense of how we could have two children with such a rare disease. Joseph's cries gave me hope as they rushed him away. I thought maybe there was still a possibility they had been wrong.

That wait was excruciating.

He was gone for an hour, and in that hour, he had already outlived his older brother. He lived for six more hours.

When they brought him back to me, despair swallowed me whole. I realized I was going to have to do it all over again. I would have to watch this precious baby take his final breath as I held him in my arms.

I was so broken. I held him for hours, even after he passed away. I did not want to let go. I knew this was the only time I would get to hold him on this side of heaven, and I wanted to hang on to every moment I could get with him.

I was in physical pain from the birth, but the real devastation was in my heart. I was exhausted. I was in shock. I was heartbroken. My spirit was absolutely crushed, and I wanted to die on that table. I didn't yet know how to process what was happening.

I wanted to scream, "What do You want from me, God?"

I am determined and often strong-minded, and nobody was going to take Joseph from me until I was ready. Because everyone in the room had been with us before, they gave me the space to do what I needed to do—to say goodbye in my own way, even if it was a long goodbye.

And then, after holding him for several hours, I suddenly knew, just as I had known with Jonathon, it was time. I felt the Holy Spirit whisper, "It is OK to let him go."

I sensed the gates of heaven open, and I surrendered my heart and let Joseph go. In that moment, I had peace. It felt supernatural, and that sense of peace is how I knew it was OK to finally let go.

Losing my boys was difficult, but that second time changed me. It crushed my spirit. I couldn't even begin to comprehend why God would allow this to happen.

TROY

We again had a lot of support when Dr. Bennie gave us the news that the baby wouldn't survive. There were a lot of people—pastors, friends, family—there to support us. As a man, I didn't want to cry. I wanted to protect my wife, even though I was dealing with my own emotions. I wanted to yell. I wanted to curse. I was angry, but I didn't show any of it.

At the time, I just thought, "This cannot be real." I was numb. I was hurt and disappointed, so I did what I had been doing the entire time—I pushed my emotions further down.

Most women do not do that, but men are often taught

to push their emotions aside. And that was precisely what I did. I didn't want to feel any of it.

Dr. Bennie and the medical team took Joseph away to run tests. He was gone longer than Jonathon, and it was different when they brought him back.

Tracy just held him and would not let him go. Even after he passed, she would not let him go. She held him for a long time.

Then, all of a sudden, she started asking all of us in the room, "Do you see the light? Do you hear that?"

My mother thought she was hallucinating, and then, out of the blue, she said, "Take the baby. It's time." After all those hours holding him, it was done, just like that.

To this day she still thinks she saw an angel and that she gave our Joseph directly to God, because when she handed him over, the atmosphere was so calm and peaceful. It was the Holy Spirit in the room with us that day.

The whole experience was different from before. You could feel the peace. It was like the calm in the middle of a storm. Something kept calming and assuring Tracy, even though we all thought the pain would be worse the second time around. Only God could have brought that level of peace in those circumstances.

For me, the second time was much harder. I was so angry. I didn't know if God really was good. All the while I was trying to be strong as a father and husband.

I was experiencing both denial and defiance. "Why us? Why twice?" I wanted answers.

Most couples don't survive losing one child; we lost two. It is a miracle we are still married.

I spent the next few days in the hospital recovering. My friend Trudy had the hospital linens made up beautifully, and my friend Erin brought me peonies. I spent a second Mother's Day in the hospital after losing a baby.

Losing a second baby was more than I could process. I was numb. Everyone was still trying to love and support us, but I didn't want anything. I was beyond devastated, and the anger began to set in. I couldn't believe God would let this happen to us again.

Leaving the hospital was like living the sequel of a bad movie. We were still displaced from Hurricane Katrina and were living in a tiny apartment because we were between homes. Troy was still trying to rebuild the business. We were digging out from underneath so much, and on top of everything, we would be going home without a baby for the second time.

I couldn't handle the thought of walking through those doors again with nothing, so we brought a dog home with us. I didn't have a baby; I had a dog. I was crushed for Josh and Abigail.

And I was done.

There was no way I was going to carry another baby in this lifetime. My dream of having more children died with that second goodbye. I didn't want any of it anymore.

Chapter 10

INTO the DARKNESS

Blessed be the God and Father of our Lord Jesus Christ, the Father of mercies and God of all comfort, who comforts us in all our affliction so that we will be able to comfort those who are in any affliction with the comfort with which we ourselves are comforted by God.

—2 CORINTHIANS 1:3–4

tracyduhon.com/videos/ch10

THE FIRST FEW months after we returned home was a really dark time in my life. I was broken and angry—at God especially. He asked me to be faithful and trust Him, so I did. But He let us go through that unspeakable pain all over again. I couldn't make sense of it. Why did this have to happen—*again*? The more I thought about it, the angrier I became. *Why?*

With Jonathon the thing that kept me going after our return from the hospital was the opportunity to honor him and celebrate his life with a huge service. The funeral was beautiful, and it truly was a celebration. But with Joseph I couldn't do it. I couldn't function. I was empty.

My spirit was crushed. I couldn't even bring myself to go to his grave. I didn't want to see where they buried him. There was a small service, but the last time I saw him was in the hospital. I couldn't do any of it. Meme helped with all the arrangements. I just wanted to disappear and be alone with my thoughts, my anger, and my numbness.

In my mind I kept reliving the hours after his birth over and over. No matter how hard I tried, I couldn't think of a scenario where any of it made sense.

I cried so much during that time I thought my face would never look normal and the tears would be a permanent fixture on my cheeks. I kept looking at pictures and videos taken when I was pregnant with Joseph because they were all I had left of him. I thought if I stopped looking at them and reliving those moments, it would be as if none of it had happened, as though he never existed.

My heart was crushed, and my arms ached to hold my baby. The pain became overwhelming. I begged God, "Make it go away!"

As I said, this was a very dark time for me. I felt my dreams were shattering and my hopes for my family were disappearing alongside them. It took me back to that hopeless place I lived in before I surrendered my life to Jesus, when I was trying to control my life.

I prayed, "Lord, promise me this is not for nothing."

I thought about the years Troy and I spent partying and abusing drugs and alcohol, and I convinced myself it was my fault that our sons developed Potter syndrome. I believed those lies because I was in so much pain. I would sit and think, "I have loved and served the Lord. I had faith for my children despite the circumstances. I am living for Christ, not the way we once lived. Yet here I am going through a mother's worst nightmare."

I began to wonder if I would be better off giving up on Jesus and going back to living for myself. I could do whatever I wanted to do. I could check out completely and retreat from life. I figured God could save His own people. I didn't want to try anymore.

The one place I would talk to God was in the shower. I would cry out in anger, "What do You want from me? God, why? Why did You let this happen?"

May 12, 2006

We don't understand. We are all frustrated because we don't have the answers, and we will remain frustrated until we ultimately give it up to the Lord and say, "It is too big for me to carry, Lord, but I trust You." The day is coming when I will understand.

My heart's cry: "Please help me!" My sadness this morning has been great, and I told Troy in the 9:00 a.m. hour that I needed to know this is not for nothing. I said, "Honey, you promise it is not for nothing." Lord, promise me this is not for nothing.

Much as it was after Jonathon, the only thing that brought me any sense of normalcy and peace in the months that followed Joseph's passing was taking care of Josh and Abigail. Loving them gave me life. For a while they were the only things I was living for.

I would yell at God, asking why we didn't get our miracle, why He needed to take both of our boys. The more I pleaded, the angrier I got because the answers never came.

I had always relied on my faith in tough times, and I knew I wasn't supposed to grieve like those who have no hope (1 Thess. 4:13), but for the first time in my life, what I was doing didn't satisfy me. When the answers didn't come in the way I wanted or needed them to, all I could do was listen and wait. I had no scriptures. I had no praise or worship songs. I just listened. And I heard the Lord whisper, "Be faithful with what is in your hands."

God was working, even though I couldn't feel Him. He heard me when I cried out to Him. He just didn't respond in the way I wanted Him to.

Even those sentiments made me angry. I cried out, "What is in my hands?" At times I didn't think I had it in me to mother the children I did have. I knew Josh and Abigail were in my hands, but the pain of losing my boys made me feel so empty.

It took four months for me to heal physically from the birth, but the emotional pain would linger for much longer. The brokenness and anger were all-consuming. By the grace of God I was able to dig deep and mother Josh and Abigail, but that was the *only* thing I did. They were my sole reason for getting up each day.

I cried all the time. Everything was a trigger. I was asking all the same questions I had after Jonathon: What did I do? What did *we* do? I had to learn to live from one moment to the next, or I would have driven myself crazy. I simply put one foot in front of the other and focused on handling only what was right in front of me.

I saw the same blank stares in the faces of friends and family after we lost Joseph, only they were magnified the second time around. People really didn't know what to say or do, not even my own mother.

I felt so isolated and alone, and that frustrated me even more. People meant well, but their words fell short. At church several people kept trying to tell me not to let the evil one steal my joy or my faith. They would give me scriptures, but I simply didn't want to hear it because it just made me angrier. The more they insisted, the more I retreated. Scripture was the last thing I wanted to hear. I knew the Word, but at that time, I couldn't feel anything but pain.

I couldn't see beyond my hurt, and I questioned whether God even had a plan for my life. I've heard a thousand times that God uses broken people to bring others to Him and show them the kingdom. But when people would try to comfort me with those sentiments, I wanted to scream.

God was working, even though I couldn't feel Him. He was pulling at my heart, drawing me close. He heard me when I cried out to Him in the shower. He just didn't respond in the way I wanted Him to. Instead of telling me why He didn't miraculously heal my boys, He simply said, "I chose you."

"Chose me for what? For this?" I didn't care how harsh I sounded. Whatever "this" was, I didn't want to be chosen for it. I wanted no part of whatever God had planned.

TROY

Everything was different after Joseph. Coming home was so difficult. I couldn't make sense of what had happened for myself, yet I felt an enormous weight on my shoulders to explain it to Tracy and to the children. That was the worst part, trying to make sense of it for them when I didn't even understand it myself.

I kept telling the kids that God is good. I said all the "Christian" things, but even the kids had questions. If God is so good, why would He allow this? I wanted to be strong, to be the man they all needed me to be. Inside I was screaming, "*Why?*"

I felt as if something was wrong with me. I wanted to take away the pain, but I couldn't, and that made me feel like a failure as a man and as a husband and father.

We were all going through so much during those months—the questions, the doubts, the anger. I watched my wife, a beautiful woman of faith, go through the hardest experience any woman can go through—carrying a baby for nine months knowing you are going to have to bury him. It seemed cruel for God to have her experience that.

As Christians, we are called to walk by faith. We believe in miracles and the healing power of God, but when there is no miracle, the pain is enormous. I believed God would never let us go through something like that again. I professed His Word and held on to faith. And then it happened again.

Twice we went to the hospital, and twice we returned home empty-handed. Twice we had to bury a child. It was something I felt no family should have to endure.

COMMUNITY

That first year after losing Joseph was the worst. Our friends and family gathered around us, doing all they could to help. They were trying to love us and nourish us spiritually. They knew I couldn't do it for myself, so they stepped in and helped me in that season, but it wasn't easy.

I would go from feeling normal to broken, swinging between the two from one day to the next. I barely even knew what "normal" was. Nothing was like it was before the boys. I was on an emotional roller coaster as I tried to navigate this new life.

The friends who were there for me during the darkest moments were absolute angels, the hands and feet of Jesus. Our church community brought us food and helped me care for my children. Another friend who had also lost a baby empathized with me through the tears and despair. They loved me when I couldn't love myself. They were there to love my children when I was a shell of the mother I knew I needed to be.

My friend Erin helped Troy pick out a beautiful canary ring for me as a Mother's Day gift. For me it signified the beauty of our sons. To this day it is one of my most cherished possessions.

My sister Glenda would drive to the house almost daily to sit with me and drink coffee. She would listen as I cried, and she would cry with me.

It made a world of difference to know there were people willing to sit with us in our grief and love us through our suffering. I think back on those

You can't go through tremendous loss or any type of major transition in your life without it changing you.

months, and I am beyond grateful for the people who surrounded us during that time. I can't imagine going through any of that alone.

I pray you have people in your life who will support you as well. We need community. We need to do life with others. We weren't meant to be all alone. If you don't have friends, family, or a good church home, I want to challenge you to be intentional about building community. We all need to actively choose to do life with others. We need to nurture relationships with people who will show up for us in times of grief and moments of joy.

I never realized just how much I needed all those people until they were carrying our burden *with* us— they were surrounding, encouraging, guiding, and lifting us up.

They were also challenging me, though they did it carefully. They knew I was hurting and needed to go through my grieving process, but they were also pushing me to believe *I was not going to die on this mountain.*

I had built so many walls around myself, thinking my anger could protect me from feeling the weight of my pain. I knew I needed to let God take me through the process to get to the promise, but that is easier said than done. Walking through it takes time. It is messy, it is emotional, and it is ugly.

It wasn't an easy journey to go on, and I know I never would have made it to the other side had it not been for my community. I placed a lot of weight on their shoulders during that time. They helped me do daily life, and they were my saving grace.

There were also people in our lives who didn't want to walk with us during that time. Trying to comprehend what we had gone through was too much for them. They made me cherish my friendships even more, because they helped me see who actually had the capacity to walk with us through adversity.

There were other people who thought I should just get over it. You never get over losing a child.

It took me three years to dig myself out, but eventually it got easier to get out of bed. I began to experience moments of joy. As I put one foot in front of the other, minutes passed, then days, then months, then years.

There would always be a missing piece—two missing pieces—but a new sense of normal began to set in. And I began to see the Lord restoring me.

One of the nurses who was at Joseph's birth found out she was pregnant, and I cooked a meal for her. It was a small gesture but also an enormous one for me. I was able to see beyond my grief and love her as I had been loved. Through small acts of service such as that one, I began to see and love myself again.

You can't go through tremendous loss or any type of major transition in your life without it changing you. At the end of those three years I felt as if I was stepping into a new version of myself. I didn't go looking for it. It just happened. I was beginning to hope again.

Although the births of our boys didn't turn out the way we hoped they would, something unexpected came from them. I developed a desire to help. I wanted to serve. God was breathing life into something bigger than me or even my family. I was beginning to find my purpose.

Chapter 11

TWO by TWO

You will have a double portion.

—Isaiah 61:7

tracyduhon.com/videos/ch11

D R. BENNIE SUGGESTED I get a hysterectomy. I don't know why the thought of doing so bothered me so much, but I had a strong reaction to it. I was advised not to have any more children, but surgery seemed so final and permanent. I would be slamming a door shut, never to open it again.

It made sense. I had just lost two babies. I was thirty-eight years old when Joseph was born. For the three years that followed, all I did was grieve and heal. Now I was in my forties. I thought there was no way I would ever carry another baby, but to hear the word *hysterectomy*—I just couldn't come to terms with it. Somewhere inside my heart I was still hoping for a miracle despite the odds, another girl so Abigail would have a sister.

I would *not* have a hysterectomy! I was adamant. It wasn't happening—period.

Dr. Bennie knew me well enough to know when I made up my mind about something, there was no convincing me otherwise.

After we lost Jonathon, our hearts were opened to the idea of adoption, and we started the process. We had friends who had been through it, and we knew it could be a lengthy process, so we wanted to put things in motion. Adoption had never been on either Troy's or my radar before Jonathon, but as I mentioned, losing a child changes you.

We had been matched with a child around the time

I found out I was pregnant with Joseph, but because we were expecting, we were taken off the list. Troy had talked with the agency, telling them we had lost one baby and were at risk of losing another, but they were firm in their response. They simply couldn't do anything.

So we waited, and we prayed—for seven years.

Troy and I talked a lot about what our family might look like following the boys. We were all in with moving forward toward adoption, so we made an appointment for him to get a vasectomy. I was forty-two and against getting a hysterectomy, but we agreed that it made sense for Troy to go ahead with the vasectomy.

He was scheduled to be in New York City for work, so I decided to go with him. He would have the procedure shortly after returning home.

It was a beautiful and much-needed trip, just the two of us. We joked around—it was our way of making light of the procedure to come. As Troy would say, "We decided to swing the bat" one more time.

We were well into the process of adoption, we had already lost two babies, and I was in my forties. I had accepted the fact that I would not have any more babies, but it was fun for those few days to imagine. I didn't think anything would come of it, but it was fun to hope.

During those years of healing and praying, I carried with me the idea of God rebuilding me and our family.

I was convinced we were supposed to adopt a baby girl, and she would be our miracle. After the pain of losing the boys, God would restore our family and bring us a little girl.

I saw a video at church about international adoption, and it stirred something inside me. China grabbed ahold of my heart. She was there. I sensed it.

It was 2009. Josh was in seventh grade, and Abigail was in fourth. I was traveling a lot because they were on the speech and debate teams, and with all their activities, it was a busy time. I was a hands-on mom, devoted to my children. I was so thankful to be there with them, especially after the boys.

After all the surgeries and health issues I faced, I started focusing more on developing healthy habits—eating well and the like. I was taking care of myself, but it became more difficult with all the traveling. I kept gaining weight and was feeling exhausted, even irritable. There were times I was so tired I would have to lie down, which was completely out of character.

I didn't know what was happening to my body. I thought it must be adrenal fatigue or perimenopause, so I made an appointment to get my hormone levels checked. I was right at that age, and it made sense, given my symptoms. I had talked with so many friends about the changes that happen to a woman as she starts to go through menopause that I had convinced myself that's what was happening to me. It was time.

When I made the appointment, it didn't even dawn on me that it was May 6, the date Jonathon went to heaven. I simply made a note in my calendar and didn't think about it again.

Dr. Bennie had walked with our family through so much that when I went into his office, we talked like two old friends. We agreed that it must be menopause, but he had to ask, "Is there any chance you could be pregnant?"

"Absolutely not!"

I was convinced there was no way I could possibly be pregnant. This was my body changing and the early stages of menopause. There was no other reasonable explanation. Plus, I knew a pregnancy at that point would be extremely high-risk and could cost me my life. So there was just no way—period.

Dr. Bennie had to follow protocol and run my blood work just to be sure, but we both knew what he would find. I was entering *menopause*.

The kids were in the waiting room while I was with the doctor, and when I saw his ultrasound technician's face, I knew something was up.

I knew God could do the impossible.

"You're pregnant!"

I experienced every emotion you can possibly imagine. I couldn't believe it. A part of me couldn't even begin to wrap my head around it, while another part of me was thrilled at the miracle I saw unfolding before my very eyes. Then, just as quickly as my heart was filled with joy, I remembered Jonathon and Joseph. My emotions were all over the place.

I knew God could do the impossible, but I also knew this baby could also develop Potter syndrome. I did not want to experience that ever again. I couldn't. I didn't think I could survive losing another baby.

Dr. Bennie was shocked but also encouraging. He reminded me to take it one day at a time. He covered me in prayer and supported me as he always had. He knew I was high-risk and had already lost two babies. We were looking at extraordinary circumstances, dangerous even.

When I left the examination room, I was in complete shock. I immediately told the kids, and they were excited. As soon as I got to the car, I called Troy to tell him. I was crying, so it was hard to get the words out.

He was silent for a moment before responding, "How did that happen?"

I said, "Well, darling..."

We laughed and cried, and at that moment, we forgot about everything that had happened before. We forgot about all the pain, the hurt, the anger, the loss. In that moment, we just felt joy. It was unbelievable.

Next, I called my friends Heather, Jennifer, and Lisa. They had been there for me through the worst, and I wanted to celebrate this with them. I was only about eight weeks along, and I knew it was premature to share the news because anything could go wrong, but I also felt this was all God.

We decided to invite Troy's mom, Meme, over to the house to talk with her. Troy's dad had just passed away, and before he died, he dreamed that we had a little girl. We didn't think too much about it at the time. But that memory flooded back to our minds.

When we told Meme, she was shocked—everyone was shocked—and then excited. We had all endured so much over the past five years—the boys, the devastation of Katrina, the loss of Troy's dad. Being able to feel joy again was healing **Even in the face of that fear, we knew we could have hope.** for us all. It was such a beautiful time. But it was an unnerving time too.

We all knew the risks. We didn't have to say anything. We knew the probability. Yet even in the face of that fear, we knew we could have hope. So we chose to hope.

We were still waiting to hear about the adoption as well. I went to the nursery and prayed. I had prayed for all my children, and I started to pray for this baby and the child God might bring into our lives through adoption and allow us to love.

Life looked so different from my original plan, but

God's plan was slowly beginning to reveal itself. That night as I prayed for all my children, I began to see it. I began to feel it—hope rising. I was trusting my heavenly Father with everything I had.

We waited to do the ultrasound until I was around nineteen weeks along. We had been at this juncture before. I just held my breath and kept holding on to hope. It was all any of us could do.

The room was filled with family, friends, and our pastors, and everyone knew the stakes were high. Nobody was going to let us do this alone. Dr. Bennie and his technician, Karen, did the ultrasound. We prayed as we waited for what seemed like an eternity. We were all holding our breath, wondering, "Will there be kidneys and a bladder?" This wasn't just any ultrasound, and everyone in that room knew it.

Karen was using extra precision, looking for details, for confirmation. She was circling where everything was: "This looks like the bladder; this is where the kidneys would be." She was very thorough and so helpful. We weren't completely in the clear, but there was hope.

We let out a collective breath. We would have to wait another few weeks to confirm with certainty that there was no sign of Potter syndrome, but for the time being we could all breathe.

Around the same time, I had an overwhelming sense that something wasn't right in our home. I had a team of people come to check it out, and as I suspected, we had mold.

It was quite common for mold to develop in areas affected by a hurricane the magnitude of Katrina, but I was surprised at the levels of mold and how long it would take to properly fix the issue. We would have to move out and rent a house for an entire year.

We found a place on Sunset, and that is where we called home for the next twelve months. It would also be where our miracle unfolded.

When we went back in for our next appointment, Dr. Bennie confirmed that the baby had kidneys and a bladder and was a healthy girl! That was the first hurdle. We had to turn our focus from the potential of Potter syndrome to my body actually being able to carry this baby.

The Lord loves to show off, and this was absolutely one of those moments. Our hearts were so full of joy, hope, and even laughter.

I had been high-risk with each of my previous pregnancies. She was my fifth and easiest. I was nauseated for about fourteen weeks, but other than that I had a healthy and normal pregnancy—no bleeding, no bed rest, none of the previous issues. I felt great.

The only concern throughout the pregnancy was how I would carry her, as she was proving to be the biggest baby yet. Day by day and month by month we watched her grow. Dr. Bennie couldn't believe it himself. He said, "I am seeing a medical miracle unfold before my eyes!"

The Lord loves to show off, and this was absolutely one of those moments. Our hearts were so full of joy, hope, and even laughter.

Here was our miracle.

In moments of silent prayer or quiet contemplation, I often think back to that time in our lives—the enormous pain followed by a season of waiting. The wait prepared us for God's great plan for our life—for our miracle—but waiting is hard. When your heart is hurting, it can often feel as though the wait will never end.

If God is asking you to wait for something, I challenge you to take some time and reflect on how the wait can prepare you for what God wants to do in your life. God is always up to something. He never wastes a moment.

Sometimes we don't even know what we are waiting for, but God is faithful and will always reveal Himself in His perfect timing. This fifth pregnancy was God's revealing Himself to us.

When I went in to deliver, we had the support of our friends and family once again. The baby was measuring so big Dr. Bennie recommended I have the C-section two weeks early.

We all knew that even though the ultrasounds looked good, things could change or something could go wrong. We decided not to do genetic testing or run any additional tests. We left it all in God's hands. He had already brought us this far.

Troy and my mother were both with me again. I was praying just as I had done with my other children, and when Dr. Bennie delivered her, she was even bigger than we thought. She was our nine-pound miracle, and she was perfect in every way. I couldn't believe it.

I was overcome with emotion and so overjoyed that she was here and healthy. My heart was bursting with gratitude as they laid her on my chest. Her face was next to mine, and she was breathing. *Thank You, Jesus.*

We had our long-desired miracle, our redemption after our suffering: Avah Hope.

TROY

We were advised not to attempt to have another child. The first ultrasound was a celebration. But when they confirmed she had all her organs, it was a whole other ball game. We erupted with joy.

That was our miracle.

Delivering Avah was such a different experience from delivering the boys. There was hope and joy in that delivery room. There was celebration and a feeling of redemption—a newness of life.

Dr. Bennie called her the miracle child because she just wasn't supposed to happen. We weren't supposed to have a healthy baby after two with Potter syndrome. The odds were stacked against us, but it did happen, and it was amazing!

During my pregnancy I had confided in my friend Erin that one of my desires was to breastfeed. I had never nursed before, but I had wanted to do so with this baby.

When Troy announced Avah's arrival, everyone was overjoyed that we had a healthy baby girl. Amid all the celebrating Erin came into my room and demanded everyone leave. She said, "We are going to nurse this baby!"

Erin is like Troy but in a dress. She took the reins and stayed in there with me until Avah latched on and fed. That was like another miracle in and of itself.

I nursed her for fifteen months.

I was so happy during those days in the hospital with our little girl. I wasn't prepared for the surge of emotions that came over me as we were preparing to go home. Finally, I was able to hold our baby *and* leave the hospital with her.

As that reality sank in, everything we experienced with the boys flooded to mind, and I was a mess. Seven years of my life culminated in that moment as I held our beautiful Avah.

I held my boys just as I was holding her, but I had to let them go. I never set foot out of my room, much less the hospital, with them in my arms. Yet here I was, leaving with this baby girl. I didn't have to let her go.

I knew this was God answering my prayers, showing me whom He needed me to love.

As we left the hospital, joyous tears of gratitude met with the deep pain of all we had endured with the boys. When we arrived back home, I was still crying. Each time I held her, nursed her, changed her diaper, I cried. It was the greatest joy.

But God wasn't done just yet. We brought Avah home in December 2010, and eighteen months later, in July 2012, we got a call that changed our lives.

"You have been matched!" the voice on the other end of the line said.

I began to pray for this little one, just as I had the others. I knew this was God answering my prayers, showing me whom He needed me to love. I had a beautiful baby girl in my arms, yet I was burdened for this little one half a world away, in China.

She was only three days old when she was left outside the orphanage on October 18, 2011. She and Avah were exactly ten months apart.

I wanted her home with us the very next day, but I knew I would have to wait. There were a lot of logistics to sort out and plans that needed to be made, and during those months, I did what I had done for all my children. I loved and mothered her the best way I knew how: I prayed.

We left for China three months later to bring home our beautiful little girl, Annahstasia Grace Song Duhon. God's plan was beautifully revealing itself day by day—two daughters, one miracle. Against all odds my dreams were coming to pass.

Chapter 12

The HEART

Things which eye has not seen and ear has not heard, and which have not entered the heart of man, all that God has prepared for those who love Him.

—1 CORINTHIANS 2:9

tracyduhon.com/videos/ch12

OUR TIME IN China changed me.

I was forty-five and the mother of what basically amounted to twin girls since they were so close in age. I had always dreamed of having two girls close in age like my sister and me, so this part of the story was like a dream come true.

Annah was beautiful, and I was overjoyed to have the opportunity to love and mother her. But my heart still ached for all I couldn't unsee and unfeel while we were in China. I had a mix of emotions and so much to process.

Each time I looked at Annah, I couldn't help but think of how different her life might have been had she not come to our family. I kept seeing the faces of the other children, those left behind at the orphanage. My heart ached.

I knew the people working at the orphanage were doing the best they could with the resources they had available to them, but it just didn't seem like enough. There had to be something more.

I had lost two children and still carried that pain with me. While you couldn't visibly see the scars, they will forever be embedded in my heart. But that very pain is what propelled me.

Our home was full of love and life. The girls were growing, and our two older children were thriving. Yet God kept stirring something inside me. I knew I had to listen and follow where He was leading me.

Everything kept pointing back to China.

I knew from losing the boys that God takes us through processes and leads us on journeys. My experience in China felt similar. I wasn't trying to force anything, but I knew I wanted to help. The desire was simple yet profound.

From the time I said goodbye to Jonathon, I felt a deep desire to help others. Whether it was cooking a meal or talking to someone about loss, I had a longing to connect to people who were hurting. I realized that by helping others, I was also healing the pain that lingered inside me. My heart was already in it, so I listened to the Lord to hear what He was trying to tell me.

My experience in China was like a shock wave straight through my heart, reaching the aching parts that still felt tremendous loss and carried that pain. It stayed with me, and would stay with me. It had a hold on me.

We were in China for a total of sixteen days. Those sixteen days would eventually change the entire direction of our life.

When we left for China, I was walking in faith. I had a peace that only God could provide, but it was still hard. Avah was almost two years old, and I had to leave her to travel across the world to get her sister. The thought of leaving her brought so much to the surface.

I had processed losing the boys through her; she was my redemption, the miracle we had prayed for. I didn't want to leave her. I knew it was only for a few weeks, but it still weighed on my heart. Goodbyes were never quite the same after the boys.

Avah stayed behind with Abigail, Joshua, and Meme. Leaving my children was hard, but knowing our other daughter was half a world away without us was even harder. I had no idea what to expect. I simply prayed and followed the Lord by faith.

That faith walk would continue to propel me forward when we were back home.

TROY

We flew to Beijing, along with about twenty other American couples who were also adopting. When we arrived, we were given the option to go to the orphanage. Of the twenty couples only three of us chose to tour the orphanage.

Tracy was adamant we needed to go. There was no question. To this day I still remember how emotional she was as we walked through the orphanage. You don't forget an experience like that.

There were five floors, but we only made it to three of them. The last two floors were off-limits. What we saw on those first three was enough to shake us, so we couldn't fathom what might be waiting on those two remaining floors.

The tour of the three floors we were able to access was rough. Most of the kids had medical issues and were housed in pens like animals. I had never seen anything like it. While it shocked me, it did something else to Tracy.

When we were told the fifth floor was for those who were terminal, Tracy lost it. After seeing how the children were being treated, she just wanted to take all of them home. I knew we couldn't make that happen, but that is what her heart was crying to do.

This was the third time in our marriage that I felt tasked with trying to make sense of the senseless. For a woman who had lost two children, hearing of a unit with terminal children was like pouring salt into a wound. She loved all children, and seeing them in such poor conditions did something in her.

Even when Annah was in Tracy's arms, something was stirring in Tracy. I could see it. I didn't know what it would look like or where it would lead, but she wanted to help. Something broke inside her during that tour.

PLANTING SEEDS

The day Annah joined our family, it was as if I were going to the hospital again. We were nervous and excited. We had seen all the pictures of her, but that simply couldn't prepare us for meeting our daughter for the first time.

It was a powerful moment. We felt peace and calm. When they brought her to us, I just held her and called her name. We cried. She touched my face and my lips. We all just knew God picked her for us. There was no question about any of it.

Adoption was never my plan, but Troy and I felt God's presence throughout the process. We sensed that God had planned this for us long before the boys, before Avah, even before Joshua and Abigail. The whole experience was surreal and humbling.

It was a five-hour drive to the orphanage from where we were staying. In the hours leading up to meeting our daughter, I was filled with anticipation. My emotions were much different when we were leaving the orphanage.

Although I had this beautiful little girl in my arms, I couldn't shake what I had seen. As we toured the orphanage, I was shocked by what I was seeing. Those precious children, most with special needs, were kept in pens. Dogs had better living conditions.

I could not believe my eyes, and it hurt to know this is where our daughter had spent the first eleven months of her life. While I was incredibly thankful to be taking her home with me, I couldn't stop worrying about all the other children. I knew some of them would never experience a mother's embrace or the warmth of a bed. Adoption was not in their future. It was a painful reality.

I wanted to take every one of those precious children home with me, but I knew that was not possible. How could I make sense of what I was feeling? How could I just sit back and accept what I had seen? My heart was breaking. I couldn't help but think of the boys.

God, why did You bring me here?

I couldn't make sense of any of it. I looked to Troy to help me understand, but it was something beyond his comprehension. It was beyond all of us.

God kept stirring something inside me. I knew I had to listen and follow where He was leading me.

Our life back home looked so different from where our daughter came from. It made me want to get Annah as far from there as possible. I wanted her to feel the love of our family and the comfort of having a place to call home.

From the moment we got home I was so grateful for our two beautiful girls. I would hold them and just thank God for choosing me to love them. Yet there was something on my heart that wouldn't let go.

I couldn't help but see the children from the orphanage each time I put our daughters to bed or closed my own eyes to sleep. Our life was beautiful, but I couldn't stop thinking about the despair we had witnessed. I couldn't turn it off.

We had heard and read stories. We had watched videos. We were just like so many others. We thought we knew the realities that existed beyond the comfort of our life. But seeing the conditions in that Beijing orphanage firsthand brought the reality home.

The faces, the smells—all of it was permanently etched on my heart. The needs of those children were no longer a video I saw at church or an article I read over coffee.

I also knew my passion to help went far beyond China. China was just one place, and we saw just one orphanage. I knew there were thousands just like it and children who were in need all over the world.

A seed needs water.

I needed to help.

In the months following our time in China, I kept asking Troy, "What can we do?" I asked him that question over and over, and I wasn't going to stop until we figured out the answer. "How can we help?"

I knew we had the means and the desire. I just didn't know exactly what helping might look like. I presented so many different ideas to Troy, hoping to find the one that might stick. I was desperately searching for that aha moment.

Much as I had done after losing the boys, I turned to God in prayer. I gave the problem over to Him and promised to faithfully follow Him. I knew there was a reason this wouldn't let go of my heart; it was like a seed in a garden that needed to grow.

A seed needs water.

At the time, I was hosting a luncheon in my home to help battered women. I had been doing so since 2006. We gathered friends, neighbors, business associates, and others to raise money for a great cause.

Through our journey of adoption I realized how many families are praying to love a precious child in need but are unable to do so because they lack the funds. Adoption is a huge expense, and that prohibits so many wonderful families.

That luncheon inspired me. "What if we can help one child a year?" I thought.

We were already bringing people together to help women. Why couldn't we do the same for children? We could raise money to help one child find a family each year.

As I was praying and thinking about this, God gave me Ephesians 1:4–6: "In love he predestined us for adoption to himself as sons through Jesus Christ, according to the purpose of his will, to the praise of his glorious grace" (ESV).

Now we had the water the seed needed to grow.

Chapter 13

The VISION

Write the vision; make it plain on tablets, so he may run who reads it. For still the vision awaits its appointed time; it hastens to the end—it will not lie. If it seems slow, wait for it; it will surely come; it will not delay.

—HABAKKUK 2:2–3, ESV

Let's Talk

tracyduhon.com/videos/ch13

GOD WAS WORKING through both Troy and me. He gave me the heart, but he gave Troy the vision.

It began with Jonathon and continued to grow with Joseph, but it was through Annah that my heart saw what it needed to see.

The luncheon was a starting place to help other families wanting to adopt, but I wanted to do more. There was still something stirring inside my heart and guiding me to a greater purpose.

The same was happening for Troy.

We were committed to serving. By doing so, we were building a different life not only for ourselves but for our children and others. We learned to serve God by helping others—a far cry from who we were back in our wild days. It was incredible to see God's work in our lives.

We had come so far. The pain we endured helped us learn about ourselves and grow as a couple. Even more important, we learned to love well. We saw how God uses our brokenness to draw us closer to Him and prepare us to do the work of the kingdom.

We knew God had called us to do more for those around us. Troy helped establish the Food Pantry of New Orleans in 2011 after turning one of his buildings at the Toyota dealership into a soup kitchen. The idea was birthed shortly after Hurricane Katrina when Troy's father reminded him to care for his people. Troy didn't take that to mean just his employees but also our neighbors, the people of New Orleans.

We saw the devastation following Katrina firsthand. The loss was compounded for us by everything that had happened with the boys. The food pantry was the first time our pain intersected with the pain of others and led us to serve the Lord by meeting needs.

Everything was done in God's timing. Losing the boys taught me that God's plan often looks *a lot* different from mine. It gave me a passion to help those who are hurting, but it wasn't until Troy saw the vision and put a plan in motion that everything really started to come together.

When I think about God's timing, I am often reminded of the years between saying goodbye to the boys and welcoming the girls. This was another season of waiting for us, seeking God's guidance, and learning to trust His timing. We wanted to help others so badly, but the when, where, and how weren't ours to choose. We had to spend some time listening to God.

We knew God had called us to do more for those around us.

One of the greatest faith lessons I learned was to let go of my own plans and embrace those of our heavenly Father. It has been a constant lesson in trust. If you've ever had to wait for God to answer a prayer, you can probably relate.

When we are praying or waiting for something, it's easy to try to take control instead of seeking God's guidance and trusting His plan. But that only leads to frustration.

The Bible says, "Trust in the LORD with all your heart and do not lean on your own understanding. In all your ways acknowledge Him, and He will make your paths straight" (Prov. 3:5–6). When God tells me something, He doesn't let it go and keeps bringing me back to it. Often, He will confirm things three times in my life. He is so faithful to guide us so we end up where He wants us to be.

LORD, LEAD THE WAY

It had been a year since we brought Annah home from China. I was still waiting for the Lord to show us how to make a difference for the orphans in China. Until then I was trusting the process He was leading us through and was continuing to surrender my desires and plans.

I was constantly praying, "Lord, what do You need from me? What do You want from me?" I knew He had a greater purpose for all we had endured. I was just waiting for it to all come together.

Our oldest daughter, Abigail, was scheduled to go on a mission trip to Honduras with Missions.Me. I needed to be home with the two younger girls, so Troy needed to go on the trip with Abigail. He went but not without kicking and screaming. He reminded me over and over that he didn't want to go.

TROY

I made a commitment to my wife on that trip to China that we would do something to help children like the ones in that orphanage. I didn't know what that would look like or how it would come together, but I knew it was a promise I intended to keep.

We were helping locally in our community. Tracy was working on the fundraising luncheon. We were serving others. Yet even though we were helping, we sensed there was still something more. Tracy knew it and reminded me often.

A year after returning from China, our oldest daughter was scheduled to go on a mission trip to Honduras. I didn't want to go. Tracy was busy with the girls, so I went but not without letting everyone know I wasn't happy about it. I now realize God wanted me to go because that trip changed everything.

In Honduras I saw unsupervised children everywhere. Some were as young as three years old, just out on the streets. It was like nothing I had ever seen. China was one thing, but this was quite another.

It shook me to the very core.

God spoke directly to me during that trip. It was so clear! *This* was the reason I needed to go with Abigail. I finally saw it. From that moment forward I had a vision.

I called Tracy. "I know why God had me come!"

Hearing God's voice that day was all I needed to put a plan in motion. I reached out to the organizers of the mission trip and started asking questions. I wanted to learn more. A plan began to take shape, and I knew exactly what we needed to do.

So often when I look back on my life, I am amazed at God. After the boys I kept hearing the same thing over and over: "I am going to awe you."

When Troy left for that trip, I had no idea it would prove to be a defining moment for him. Once God gave him the vision, a plan came to life.

When he called me, I could tell from the minute he began speaking that something had happened. After seeing all the small children alone on the streets, some as young as our two girls, he knew immediately what he needed to do. He finally saw what I had seen in China—a need to create a place for suffering children, to give them love and a home.

On that mission trip to Honduras the idea for Hope House was born. God planted a vision in Troy to build homes for these children. That was something I had wanted for so long, but to see the seed grow in my husband was like a dream come true.

I couldn't believe what Troy was telling me. He had promised we would find a way to help children in need, but it finally felt real. I didn't know how the plan would unfold, but I knew it would happen. We were going to do this!

For as long as I could remember, this had been our dynamic. God used both our strengths to accomplish His plans. Troy would be at business meetings or large events and functions talking with people. I would accompany him and bring heart to all of it. He would inspire people through his business spirit while I would pray for people and speak God's Word. That was our strength as a couple.

After what we had seen in China, our vision was for so much more than just four walls and some bricks. We wanted to build a church, a home, a family—a community.

Troy got to work almost immediately. He reached out to Angel House, one of the organizers of the mission trip to Honduras. Angel House was already doing mission work in many countries across the globe, so it was a natural place to start. The model they used internationally inspired Troy, and he inspired them with his vision to build orphanages.

After what we had seen in China, our vision was for so much more than just four walls and some bricks. We wanted to build a church, a home, a family—a community. We wanted to build more than an orphanage; we wanted to make it a home. That was always our intention. The vision Troy saw was for homes.

We wanted the children to know the love of a family and to be in an environment anchored in faith. I wanted the homes to be like the home we were building for our children.

We already knew some children likely would never be placed, and many of them would come out of orphanages and go to the streets. We wanted all the children to have a family and know the power of having someone to call a mother or father.

I thought my heart to mother was simply for my own family, but God showed me it was so much more.

Building that first home was like having another baby for us. It was an idea birthed from our experience, the result of a journey God had taken us on. This is what God had placed on our hearts and in our minds after everything we had walked through. Building the children's homes wasn't like bringing a baby home from the hospital, but it was still something God was birthing through us and breathing life into.

I began to pray. I prayed for the process of building these homes. I prayed for the children who needed them. I prayed that God would continue to guide us.

We poured everything into this effort and saw our prayers answered in real time as one thing after another came together. The opportunity for me and Troy to create loving homes for children was both beautiful and overwhelming at times, but seeing the vision realized filled my heart with so much gratitude.

Everything we do we do as a family. This effort was no different, and there were times along the way when I couldn't help but wish the boys could be part of it. I also knew that through the work we were doing, we were living in the fullness of God's redemptive power. God was turning our pain into purpose and allowing the boys we lost to live on through the vision of the Hope homes.

As we got closer to the opening of that first house, I was so thankful to God. Not only could I feel Him changing me and making me the person He created me to be. I was watching Him bring His beautiful purpose out of our enormous pain.

God gave me the desires of my heart, and I was amazed that He let us be part of this extravagant plan.

I thought my heart to mother was simply for my own family, but God showed me it was so much more.

We opened our first Hope House in India exactly one year after Troy and Abigail went to Honduras. Annah was three and a half and Avah was four and a half when we opened it.

I didn't know what to expect; I just knew God was calling us to India. He needed us to get out of the boat and walk with Him on the water. We were in unfamiliar territory, and that required great trust. But the experience was powerful and surreal. It felt as if I was watching God create a masterpiece. He used us as His hands and feet to pull it all together. It was clear that He was leading; we just followed.

By taking the steps God put in front of us, He did something much bigger than us. He turned our brokenness into a mission that would change lives.

By taking the steps God put in front of us, He did something much bigger than us. He used our brokenness and pain and turned it into a mission that would change lives. The Hope House in India was the culmination of everything we had gone through—the boys, all those years loving Josh and Abigail, the miracle of Avah and Annah, Troy and me as a couple. It was beautiful. It was extravagant. It was what God called us to do.

When Hope House became a reality, it showed me that our capacity to love isn't finite. I didn't even realize it until we were there. That is what God wanted me to see—He needed me to open my heart and love others as He loved them.

And it didn't stop in India.

Chapter 14

LOVING WELL

For I was hungry and you gave me something to eat, I was thirsty and you gave me something to drink, I was a stranger and you invited me in, I needed clothes and you clothed me, I was sick and you looked after me, I was in prison and you came to visit me.

—Matthew 25:35–36, NIV

Let's Talk

tracyduhon.com/videos/ch14

INDIA WAS JUST the beginning. When Troy returned from Honduras, the thing he knew beyond a shadow of a doubt was that there couldn't be just one home. The plan was to build one orphanage each year. So the fundraising luncheon, which became known as Hope for Children, would help one child each year find adoptive parents, and through Hope House we would build one children's home each year. It was a massive undertaking, but one Troy was determined to accomplish.

We began Giving Hope with the work we were doing after Katrina. We were feeding people and providing meals through our food pantry, touching the lives of nearly three thousand people per week. Everything just grew from there.

We partnered with the New Orleans Mission and funded the Giving Hope Retreat Center, a sixty-acre facility that helps rehabilitate drug addicts and alcoholics, and provides shelter and work for many of the homeless throughout the city and surrounding area.

We continued to raise money through Hope for Children, which impacts dozens of children each year and has supported over twenty adoptions. We also opened the Giving Hope Community Center, a facility that offers a variety of programs for the Desire neighborhood and surrounding communities, including summer camps and job training.

Everything we were doing was to share the love of Christ and show people how He can change everything. The work God had called us to with Hope House filled my soul and nurtured me. It inspired me to step into this new space and grow into the person I am today.

Opening the home in India in the summer of 2014 allowed fifty children to sleep in a bed, celebrate special events such as birthdays, and have clean water for the first time in their lives. When the vision came to life, it was as if all my hopes as a little girl to nurture children and my grown-up experiences as a mother were magnified.

Each of us has a story, something God wants to use. Those stories hold great power, as they can inspire us and create great change.

After we opened the home in India, Hope House just kept expanding.

At home our doors were open to friends, neighbors, and children who interacted with my kids. We were modeling in our home the same sense of community we were building through Hope House and the other outreaches.

I remember one young woman who came to us after she'd been through a rough patch in her life. I hired her to work for me, and as we got to know each other, I could see that there was a missing piece in her life. I found myself mothering her; it was just what I did.

That was my heart. She nicknamed me Mama T, and it just sort of stuck.

MOTHER OF MANY

Motherhood looked so different from what I had imagined all those years ago. I had devised my own plan for my life, but I was discovering that God had other plans for what motherhood would look like for me. I finally came to a place where I could surrender my will to God and accept that my vision wasn't going to work out the way I thought.

Being a mother was my heart. But God used the loss of my children to grow something I wasn't expecting. Losing my boys only deepened my desire to mother. Out of my broken heart God built something beautiful— a passion to mother many. The children may not all have lived in my home, and I may not have given birth to them, but I wanted to be part of their lives.

God used the loss of my children to grow something I wasn't expecting.

The children who called each Hope House home truly held a place in my heart. I prayed for them as I did my children and loved them as though they were all part of our family.

This is the strength and beauty behind Hope House—the power of belonging, the power of family.

In 2015 our team went back to where it all began for Troy: Honduras. We helped construct a new boarding school called Plan Escalon. The facility is home to over six hundred orphans and at-risk students in junior high and high school.

We sent two teams to plan the opening. One helped with the construction of the dorms and facility; the other led the celebration when the facility was completed and volunteered in a mountain village with some of the students.

Honduras continues to be one of our largest facilities to date.

During the summer of 2016 we traveled to Gambia to open our third Hope House. And in 2018 a team of sixteen people crossed the arctic circle to open our fourth, in Kolomna, Russia, just outside Moscow. That Hope House now stands as a model for orphanages across Russia and is being replicated.

Brazil was our fifth location. We traveled there in 2018 and met the Torres family. They own 50 percent of the water supply distributed throughout Brazil and fund over five hundred missionary families. They too wanted to help change lives in their community.

Troy met with them to explore how we could work together to help children and families in need. Through the partnership with the Torres family, we were able to create a community center in one of the poorest areas of Brazil, a region where drugs were rampant. And there were plans to create more jobs within the community.

The community center and church would be a place where kids could learn and their mothers could have a job that paid more than they could earn working on the farms. We wanted to change an entire community through the work we would do with the Torres family.

When the plans were first coming together, we often used translators because I couldn't understand much of what was being said. Troy was in the middle of talking with them about the plans when a woman pulled me aside and began to speak prophetically.

There in Brazil this woman I had never met prophesied that I would be a "mother of many." She knew nothing of what I had been through or my heart to be a mother. My calling was bigger than loving people in my home and our inner circle; my purpose was to love all God's children.

When I think of how much has changed since those months when I didn't know if I would be able to crawl out of the darkness, I am in awe of what God has done. The Lord told me, "I called you a 'mother of many'; you don't get to choose what that looks like." I didn't choose the work we have done in our community and around the world. God chose it for me. This was the purpose He put on my heart. God needed me to mother, so that is what I did.

CHANGE MAKER

> Speak out; judge righteously; defend the rights of the poor and needy.
> —PROVERBS 31:9, NRSVUE

The Brazil home opened in 2019 and made an immediate impact in that community. That project truly put our work to change lives on a grander scale.

Each orphanage is home to thirty to fifty children. Troy's goal is to build twenty orphanages in twenty years, allowing thousands of children across the globe to feel the warmth of home and the love of God.

To serve others is to love others.

A home in the Dominican Republic was set to open in 2020, right before the world all but shut down during the pandemic. We had to put that project on hold, but it finally opened in 2021.

The South Africa Hope House opened in 2022, followed by a Family Crisis Center in Ukraine in 2023. A partnership in the Philippines is in the works for 2024, and we still desire to go back to China and build something there.

With each Hope House, my capacity to love grows more and more. I see all these beautiful children whom

169

I get an opportunity to pray for, mother, and love, and I am reminded of my boys. It is a way for me to honor them.

I have watched people across the globe open their hearts to children in need, a constant reminder that we all have the capacity to love others. No matter our circumstances or experiences, we all have the ability to open our hearts and love others well. We can all do *something*. It can be as simple as serving a meal or as grand as building an orphanage in another country. Whatever form it takes, to serve others is to love others.

We all have something that can be healed through loving others.

Through the work we are doing and the people we have met, I realized there is a passion within all of us. For me it was mothering; my loss allowed me to see that. We all have something that moves us, something that can reveal our purpose.

Each of us has a path and a story. We all have something that can be healed through loving others. What is that thing for you?

We all take the pain of our own experience and allow it to guide and fuel us. Even when you're faced with uncertainty or struggling to put one foot in front of the other, you can be someone's blessing.

When my pain seemed unbearable, I thought God had failed me. I had to find something else in order to survive. I dared to believe God was taking me somewhere.

God is good. You just need to let Him work through you. Bad things happen, but when you trust God, you get to see what He can do. I am a living witness, and I know He's not done.

Hope grows within each of us every single day. Troy and I get to witness that through the work God has called us to do.

Giving Hope has served over three million pounds of food worth over nine million dollars. We have launched eight Hope House projects, with plans for more locations.

We launched an initiative with a local partner to help combat human trafficking; we started People2Pray, which offers support and prayer to many around the country; and we started Women of Hope Unite (WOHU), a network of women dedicated to finding the gold in one another.

Founded on 1 Peter 4:10, WOHU casts vision by asking women, "What is the passion that inspires you and the injustice that angers you?" By doing this, we encourage women to use their time, talents, and treasures to create a legacy for generations to come. With a focus on four key initiatives—empowering women, supporting mental and brain health, mentoring teens, and leading Hope for Children—WOHU has significantly impacted the lives of over 440 children locally and globally in the last decade.

Meanwhile, Hope for Children has been expanded to help children across the areas of adoption assistance, foster care family support, care for critically ill children, the Giving Hope Community Center, and Legacy Gift Scholarships.

There is so much more work to do, and there will never be a shortage of people to love, help, and pray for. We can all use our stories and what we have lived through to help others, inspire change in the world around us, and build God's kingdom here on earth.

Chapter 15

REDEMPTION

I know that my Redeemer lives, and at the last He will take His stand on the earth.

—Job 19:25

tracyduhon.com/videos/ch15

IN 2017 TROY and I were at a marriage conference at Bethel Church in Redding, California. I remember it vividly. By that point we had been through so much.

We all process pain in our own way. I took to journaling and poured my heart out to God in prayer; Troy dealt with our losses very differently, and it was at that conference that I truly began to see how everything had played out in Troy's heart. He had suppressed his grief and needed to be set free. He needed to release the wound created from the loss of our sons and be revived.

At the conference, Troy and I participated in a workshop where we were led in a process of deep inner healing. The leaders weren't messing around. When they called Troy and me up for ministry, they didn't start with niceties to pass time. They went straight to the heart. It was as though they could see right through Troy and knew exactly what he needed. The workshop leaders started asking Troy questions, probing him to go deeper.

And then it happened.

In front of over 250 people, my husband let it all out. He curled up on the floor and cried out. He was finally releasing the intense pain he'd held for so long. He was letting go of the disappointment and anger that grabbed hold of his heart following the loss of our boys. His emotions were real and raw. It was a beautiful moment, one God chose specifically to heal Troy.

There wasn't a dry eye in the room that day. Everyone was crying, both men and women. Most men look for anything to distract them from the pain they feel. Watching God minister to Troy in that way was incredible and likely set others free.

When we signed up for that conference, it was simply to grow in our marriage; instead, the event freed my husband to be the man he was created to be.

Our beautiful partnership and journey together came full circle in that moment. For so long Troy wanted to protect me and felt he had failed at doing so. He carried that guilt and anger, along with the devastation of losing two boys. God healed Troy's heart at that conference, and He was about to work another miracle in our marriage.

CREATING A LEGACY

I had prayed and hoped for a miracle following the loss of the boys. I thought the girls were that miracle, but God continued to pour into our lives. By staying the course and listening to the Lord, even when it seemed impossible, we were able to bring something else to life—a ministry that has touched the lives of children in our community and around the world.

None of that would have happened if Troy and I hadn't been together. If we hadn't gotten married, we wouldn't have had the boys or girls or built the orphanages. There would have been no vision, no seeds, no plans.

God used our marriage partnership and losing the boys to create a legacy for them here on earth. We honor them in everything the Lord has allowed us to do, and they live on through the work we do—each child we help, each mouth we feed, each broken heart we meet with compassion. We are led by His Spirit to complete the mission God planted in our hearts—and it is all a testament to our boys.

Although Jonathon and Joseph were here on earth less than twenty-four hours, they are changing lives across the globe because of the impact they had on our hearts. God used them to break us and show us the world as He needed us to see it. He wanted to direct us to the places He needed us to be. He needed us to walk into the unknown and uncertain places by faith. He carried us through the hardest times in our lives and ultimately breathed life back into our marriage.

God used our pain for a greater purpose, inspiring the work we do with Giving Hope. The boys aren't gone; they are simply being held by the Father until we are all reunited in heaven.

I miss my boys. I sometimes sit in the stillness of morning and wonder what they would be interested in. Would they look more like me or Troy? How would they interact with their brother and sisters? Would they be athletic? Would they be smart? Where would their hearts lead them in this world?

Unable to touch them, I see and feel them through the work we are doing and the lives we continue to reach. Giving Hope has become the answer to all the questions. It is their legacy, and it is anchored in love—a mother's love. *God used them* to break us and show us the world as He needed us to see it.

I still don't know medically why we had two sons diagnosed with Potter syndrome, but our experience is a constant reminder that God is always in charge. The COVID pandemic was another reminder of that. While it brought some people closer, it did the opposite for many others. So many people were struggling all over the world.

In the midst of lockdowns and uncertainty, beautiful spaces were created for deep reflection. My family was home with me. We were together. During that time, I found myself thinking of the boys more and more.

I knew I needed to do something for myself, for my heart and my healing process. I poured all my thoughts and emotions onto paper. I knew the boys would never physically receive these letters, but just writing them put a piece of my heart back together. The letters made me feel as if the boys were with us in those times when we were all together as a family.

May 4, 2020

Dearest Joseph,

Today is your birthday. You would be fourteen years old and would have woken up to donuts, one of our traditions to celebrate. Your siblings love it! Donuts are so fun and yummy!

I still choose to see you through my heavenly Father's eyes, with an eternal perspective that you and your brother Jonathon are walking with your Creator and through His Son, Jesus, we are never truly apart.

Someday I will go to you and Jonathon. I hold on to the words David prayed in 2 Samuel 12:23 when his son died: "I will go to him, but he will not return to me."

For now, I want to tell you how much I miss you and how much I would love to have you here with me—to hold you, to play with you, to hug you, to mother you, and for you to be with our family. Your brother Joshua misses you more than anyone could imagine. He's been fishing and loving it and would love to have you with him.

I want to tell you the story of your life and about the mother you helped me become.

Today as I sat with our Abba Father, He filled my heart with the revelation that you have been sitting in His presence and filled with His glory for all these years I have been missing you. My heart rejoices knowing that is where you are and have been since the moment you took your last breath in my arms.

One of the hardest parts of you leaving me was that I wanted you to know my love, and it hurt my heart so much that you would not know that love. As I cried out to God, He showed me you already know my love because God is love. You sit in the presence of God—of love itself—and because of that you know Mommy's love!

Daddy and our family have the honor of living out on this side of heaven the purpose and destiny you inspired through your life. It has not been easy, but Mommy has held on to the same hope, faith, and trust in God that I had before I conceived you, while I carried you, and after I birthed you. I live by that hope, faith, and trust each day as Jesus continually heals my heart through knowing I am a part of your and Jonathon's lives. The hope I never let go of is the very life-giving hope I now live in. It has shaped my purpose and our family's, and it is the destiny your dad and I will live out until we meet you again.

My precious Joseph, you and Jonathon continue to live on and lead people closer to Christ. You have inspired us to be the hands and feet of Jesus, and your lives are both greatly connected to your siblings' lives through the redemption God has brought in our family.

You helped me to not give up and to keep believing there was a purpose for our pain, that you and your brother had a great calling and destiny. I am who I am today because I dared to believe you were both seeds of righteousness sown into the kingdom of God.

God loved me back to life, and He showed me there truly was hope and a future! He turned my pain into purpose. He showed me that when Jesus is all you have, you discover He is all you need. He gave me Daddy and your siblings to love me back to life and give me a reason to keep going.

Today I have received the promise of healing. It is evident in everything I do and who I am!

I am eternally grateful that Jesus allowed me to carry you, to feel you move and kick, and to sit for hours in prayer and worship with you. Through you I would learn to walk out my faith in a deeper way than I ever could have imagined and to do so with your brother and sisters.

You taught me to live out every part of my faith and mother you. It is just so very different than I had planned.

—MOMMY

May 6, 2020

My dearest Jonathon,

I waited for your birthday to write this note to you. You would be sixteen years old today, and not one year goes by that I do not celebrate your life and your brother Joseph's life.

Your lives bless people every day.

I had to say goodbye to you so fast. I was not prepared to let you go. I didn't want to let you go. I held you for hours. It took heaven to come to earth in our room and an angel of the Lord to tell me it was OK for me to finally let you go!

You looked just like your brother Joshua. He never got to meet you or Joseph, but he knows all about you. You would be his best friend. My heart hurts for him, as he truly misses his brothers and the life you could have all shared together, but I trust God has a beautiful plan of redemption for Joshua, and one day for all eternity you will both be with him and our family again!

You birthed in me an unshakable faith that was with me from the time when you were three months along that I was told you would not live to leave that delivery room, where I held you in my arms. I mothered you and carried you with the greatest faith of my life. You were born with that same incredible faith within you as you took your last breath and joined our Creator. I prayed you would miraculously begin to breathe again, although I knew when you did not, you were in the arms of God. Holding you was like having a piece of heaven in my arms.

After you left us, I spoke in your honor to hundreds of people, sharing the gospel and the love of God with them. Today I still share the gospel and the love of God in your and your brother Joseph's honor. It is my calling and the calling of our entire family.

The God of all hope is so much greater than we ever imagined, and it is because of you and your brother that we can live that out each day, breathing life into that hope.

Your sister Avah's middle name is Hope, and she represents redemption, which also became my life's mission and my heart's passion. In losing you, I learned to help and love others.

Your life and your brother's life led us to create Giving Hope NOLA. We were called to adopt your sister Annahstasia— I call her Promise Fulfilled—and through that experience and my desire to love all children, Hope House was birthed. There are now homes on every continent.

We are helping and loving others, and everything we do is about Giving Hope, a hope you inspired. Your legacy lives on, inspiring hope in people across the world.

As a mother, my greatest hope is to raise my children to love and live for Jesus, to know Him and make Him known, and to live out the calling and destiny God has for each of you.

Jonathon, my beautiful boy, the mission you inspired will continue until the day we meet again. I am honored and grateful to be your mom and to do this work in your honor, to honor God, and to know you are sitting with Him in heaven.

Thank you for giving me life through your life with our Abba Father!

I miss you so much, and I love you like crazy.

−MOMMY

Life has many roads and brings many challenges. We all go through them. I never could have imagined what my challenges would look like or what I would have to walk through.

When my world fell apart, I realized life isn't promised to be perfect. God took the broken pieces and put them back together. From the depths of darkness came light. From the place of hurt came hope.

God changed me, constantly pushing me toward the person He wanted me to be—the mother, woman, and wife He wanted me to be.

Because of Him alone I can finish strong. I can do the work.

And there is still work to be done.

CONCLUSION

Better is the end of a thing than its beginning, and the patient in spirit is better than the proud in spirit.

—ECCLESIASTES 7:8, ESV

Let's Talk

tracyduhon.com/videos/conclusion

Without hope I would never have made it through the tough moments. Without faith I wouldn't be who I am today.

God carried me to this beautiful place where I am inspired to use my pain to help others, lead people to Christ, and serve our Lord.

That is my greatest hope for you. I want you to find the passion that inspires you and the injustice that angers you. I want you to be so moved that you go out into the world and make a difference in the areas you feel called to.

I want you to serve a greater purpose.

We all have the ability to change the world around us. Sometimes even small gestures that seem insignificant can massively change someone's life or heart. We just have to take that first step and continue putting one foot in front of the other.

We may not understand why God opens certain doors in our lives, but when you come upon them, I want you to feel encouraged. I want you to walk through them boldly, with faith and a deep sense of trust. I pray you will allow yourself to step into a plan greater than your own.

The loss of my boys birthed in me a heart to help others, to address the injustices and do God's work in this world. That was the place God needed to bring me to, to find that strength within myself to be inspired to make a difference.

From my greatest pain came God's greatest purpose for my life, and I am forever grateful for the work He has done. I know with all my heart He can do the same for you.

TROY

There were moments throughout this journey when I was consoling Tracy that I would just dance with her. Those times when we were holding on to each other, swaying slowly, were priceless.

I didn't have the answers. All I knew to do was hold her and love her. But they were some of the most beautiful moments.

I wanted so badly to tell Tracy everything would be OK. That's what most husbands want to tell their wives. But there is nothing more sincere than just being willing to hold your wife, to simply be present and love her. That is what I did—I held Tracy. I held her because I didn't have the answers. I just had this deep love for her.

I saw my wife, this incredible woman of faith, go through so much pain. We both experienced the loss of our boys, but Tracy stepped out. She believed more than anyone.

It was Tracy who always kept the faith and had the heart. When I think back on everything that happened and the work we are doing today, the miracle is us. God was with us through it all.

Many couples would have walked away; they would have crumbled from the pressure. I held on because of Tracy. Watching her walk through the worst thing imaginable for a parent and seeing her consistently believe bigger allowed me to do the same. It pushed me to let the pain fuel our passion.

We wouldn't be doing any of what is happening today had it not been for what we walked through together. The work we do here on earth is because of our boys watching from heaven. It's all about loving well. It's that simple.

Each of us has a story, something God wants to use. Those stories hold great power, as they can inspire us and create great change.

There are endless opportunities to learn from our experiences, and when we do, we understand how beautiful each story can be, even when we've gone through horrific circumstances.

When I talk with people who are hurting and they realize the magnitude of what we endured, there is a level of openness that comes, a common thread connecting us because they can identify with the pain we walked through.

I see it in the eyes of the mother who lost a child, in the hug of a woman wishing to be a mother, in the arms of the woman desperately trying to escape the shame of her past, and even in the husband wanting to be better for his family.

From my greatest pain came God's greatest purpose for my life, and I am forever grateful for the work He has done.

No matter what we've gone through or what we've done, God wants to use our stories for His glory. There is something within each of us, within the things we've survived, that God wants to use to bring about His purpose.

That is both powerful and beautiful.

Giving Hope was birthed from our story. It is simply what we get to do—what God wanted to do through us and how He is using our story.

What does He want to do through you?

HELLO, MY NAME
IS HOPE

THE STORY YOU just read tells of a hope I never let go of. If you want to know more about the One my hope is in, scan the following QR code for a special video called *Hello, My Name Is Hope.*

Let's Talk

tracyduhon.com/videos/hope

DISCUSSION GUIDE

As you turn the pages of this book, I hope you find both hope and inspiration. It was created with you in mind, offering moments to pause and reflect on your own life.

Here are some questions to help guide you on your own journey. It is through these questions that I hope you find the purpose that inspires you, the injustices that anger you, and a greater plan revealed to you as only God can do.

- What is God trying to inspire in you through your own story?

- What is holding you back from trusting fully in God's plan for your life?

- Is there a painful experience you need to fully process and be healed of to allow yourself to truly start living again?

- In your moments of doubt, where do you turn?

- What parts of your life are you still trying to control?

- What parts of my story resonate with you the most?

- What is the first step you can take toward your healing?

- Whom has God placed in your life for you to serve as you navigate your way from pain to purpose?

- When you sit in silence, what is the thing that ignites your heart?

- What can someone else learn from your story?